New Ways of Ontology

New Ways of Ontology

by NICOLAI HARTMANN

Translated by

REINHARD C. KUHN

HENRY REGNERY COMPANY
Chicago · 1953

NEW WAYS OF ONTOLOGY is an authorized translation
of *Neue Wege der Ontologie* published in 1949
at Stuttgart by W. Kohlhammer.

Copyright 1952
HENRY REGNERY COMPANY
Chicago 4, Illinois

Library of Congress Catalogue Card No. 53-5776

Manufactured in the United States of America
CZDZEC

TABLE OF CONTENTS

New Ways of Ontology

and relations, involves an ontological prejudgment. To a much higher degree, however, this applies to philosophical interpretations of the world, determined as they are by a specific point of view.

Among historically recorded systems of philosophy there is none for which the domain of the problems of being, taken in strict universality, is not essential. The more profound among them have at all times raised the question of being, each of them seeking to answer it in accordance with its particular outlook. According to whether this question is either posed and discussed or ignored, doctrinal systems can be classified as founded or unfounded ones, regardless of their respective points of view or doctrinal tendencies. The more significant accomplishments of all periods, recognizable even to a superficial glance because of their far-reaching effect, are without exception "founded" systems.

In no way does this mean that founded systems are ontologically constructed systems or even realist ones. The great theoretical structures of German idealism illustrate this truth in the most characteristic fashion. When Fichte, in his early *Uber den Begriff der Wissenschaftslehre*, derives the being of things from creative activities of the Ego, he furnishes an answer to the question as to what the being of things is. His is a basic ontological thesis, and, as such, it is a foundation for all that follows, even down to the truly burning questions with which his *Wissenschaftslehre* is concerned—questions about man, will, and freedom.

The same holds, *mutatis mutandis*, for Schelling and Hegel in all phases of their philosophies, no matter whether the ultimate foundation of being be sought in a subconscious intelligence, in the fusion of subject and object, or in Absolute Reason. In fact, the same holds true for Kant and even Berkeley. Fundamentally though the immaterialism of the latter may differ from transcendental idealism, the thesis *"esse est percipi"* is still as much an ontological proposition as Kant's finely balanced assertion that things in space and time are only phenomena.

By their fundamental theses the idealist systems are no less ontologically constructed than the realist ones. The distinctive mark of the former, as contrasted with the latter, is that their concept of being is a derived one. And therewith they find themselves irreconcilably opposed to the tradition of the Old Ontology. This opposition is a conscious one, deliberately chosen on epistemological and ethical grounds. Further, it is an opposition which, in view of the indifference of the later idealists of the nineteenth century toward fundamental questions, led to the dissolution of the old ontology.

This dissolution marks a decisive step in the history of philosophical theories. Indeed, the dissolution did not first begin with idealism. The way was prepared for it by the typically modern trend toward an epistemological-critical foundation of philosophy, and by the end of the seventeenth century it reached its first high point in Leibniz's philosophy. This philosophy is still, in its own way, the creation of a thoroughly ontological type of thought. Yet in the main Leibniz has already left the tracks of the old ontology.

The question then arises as to what the old ontology actually was. We mean by it that theory of being which was dominant from Aristotle down to the expiration of Scholasticism. Although it produced a multitude of divergent varieties of thought and finally ran out in an incurable division of tendencies, it was uniform in its fundamentals, and to the thinkers of the modern age, who from several sides drew up a concentrated attack upon it, it presented a unified hostile camp.

The old theory of being is based upon the thesis that the universal, crystallized in the *essentia* as substantial form and comprehensible as concept, is the determining and formative core of things. Besides the world of things, in which man, too, is encased, there is a world of essences which, timeless and immaterial, forms a kingdom of perfection and higher being. The extreme representatives of this doctrine even assigned true reality to the universal essences alone, thereby disparaging the world of time and things. Their successors in the nineteenth century, considering universals only under the form of concepts, called this trend "conceptual realism." The expression is misleading, because it was the point of that theory that universals were not just concepts. Instead, one may well speak of a "realism of universals."

Scholastic ontology, far from being limited to this extreme view, showed the theory of universals in richly varying gradations. It was not necessary to attribute to essences a being "prior to things" or "above" them. They could be conceived also in the Aristotelian manner as substantial forms subsisting "in the things." Thus the difficulties of a duplication of the world were avoided without a surrender of the fundamental conception. Of course, medieval philosophers could not entirely rest content with this, because a speculative, theological interest prompted them to conceive universals as entities pre-existing in the *intellectus divinus*.

Apart from this, the gist of this ontology does not lie in the gradations of the fundamental thesis. Nor does it lie in the speculative-metaphysical tendencies combining with it but solely in the basic view of the nature of the universal itself —in the conviction that the universal is the moving and teleologically determining principle of things. Here an age-old motif of mythical thinking enters: the teleological interpretation of temporal occurrence in analogy to human action. Aristotle gave this idea a philosophical form, linking it closely to a theory of *eidos* patterned chiefly on organic nature. According to this view, essence is a substantial form, and, as the end of an evolutionary process, it determines the growth of the organism. This scheme of interpretation was transferred from the organism to the whole world, and, in analogy to the organic, all processes of inorganic nature were considered teleological.

This scheme had the advantage of solving the riddle of the structure of the world in an amazingly simple manner. If only the observer succeeds in grasping the substantial form of a thing, he holds at once the key to all the changes which it suffers. The substantial form, however, is comprehensible by means of the concept, and the methodological tool for this comprehension is the definition. Definition again is a matter of the intellect whose whole business consists in gathering the essential elements of the form from the final stages of the natural processes of growth and in then putting these elements together in an orderly fashion.

This procedure, surely, must not be conceived in the manner of a crude empiricism. The most general traits of essence, that is, those that are shared by many kinds of *essentia*, cannot simply be gleaned from a survey of things. Here the Aristotelian epistemology did not offer the right lever, and soon Scholasticism espoused the Platonic idea of intuition *(intuitio, visio)*. Philosophers became more and more used to subordinating the intellect to a superior faculty of insight to which they ascribed a direct contact with the highest ontologically determining formal elements.

Herewith the old ontology took on a deductive character. Once human reason feels itself to be in possession of the highest universals it is readily concluded that reason can actually "derive" from these universals all that which it does not know how to extract from experience. In this manner, there arose that neglect of empirical knowledge and that luxuriant growth of a metaphysics deducing its conclusions from pure concepts which was first challenged by the later nominalism and finally defeated by the beginnings of modern natural science.

It goes without saying that in as summary a discussion as the present one we cannot do justice to medieval metaphysics. But here our concern is not with medieval metaphysics but with contemporary issues. For these, it is imperative that we achieve a clear view of certain fundamental traits of the ontological views which were at the basis of that metaphysics. We must learn from the mistakes of these old ontological views, so that any and every attempt at a new ontology may dissociate itself unambiguously and consciously from all such errors.

The critical epistemology of the modern age from Descartes down to Kant did not succeed in completely replacing the old ontology with a new doctrine of equal value. But it had so thoroughly destroyed its presuppositions that a metaphysics erected on the old basis was no longer possible. The *Critique of Pure Reason*, in which the work of thorough housecleaning reached its end, marks a historical boundary beyond which ontological thinking all but vanishes. This is noteworthy, because the Kantian critique was actually not leveled against the foundations of the old ontology but rather against the speculative-rational metaphysics which had been built upon it.

In Kant it is above all the deductive mode of procedure which is done away with. Deductions can be made only from a priori certain principles, and apriorism is here subjected to a searching critique. The a priori is limited to two forms of intuition and a few categories. And even these are considered valid only for phenomena and not for things as they are in themselves. Thus substantial forms are excluded as a matter of course, and along with them the doctrine of *essentia* is obliterated. More important still is the fact that the *Critique of Judgment* attacks teleology even on its very home ground, that of organic nature, depriving it of all constitutive signifi-cance.

The latter point is perhaps the most important of all. At any rate, it hits the weakest side of the old ontology drifting in the wake of Aristotle. But surely it is the point least under-stood and valued by Kant's contemporaries and followers. The philosophies of nature of both Schelling and Hegel ig-nored the critique of teleological judgment and carried on once more in conformity with the Scholastic example. The Kantian critique had been a transcendental one, that is, an epistemological critique of the presuppositions of the theory of organic nature. Rationalist idealism, however, believed it-self to be in possession of unassailable universal certainties on the strength of which the enigmatic purposive equipment of living beings—and actually of all nature from the bottom up—is supposed to become amenable to teleological interpretation.

Chapter II

The Categories of Being

A SURVEY of this state of affairs at once clearly shows that the New Ontology can in no way consist of another resuscitation of the old one. Not only has the teleological scheme of interpretation proved untenable despite all efforts at renewal. It has become necessary, moreover, to exclude every sort of thesis which might serve as a disguise for an outdated metaphysics. That is not quite as easy as it might seem at first glance. The traditional grooves still determine modern thinking, and usually the investigator does not realize to what extent they lead him on. So in the recent past the doctrine of *essentia* experienced a rebirth in phenomenology—seemingly without any metaphysical aspiration but, in truth, not without the reappearance of very old and often conquered difficulties and not without a temptation to equally old and often censured mistakes.

It will not do to approach the new doctrine of being as an "ontology of essences." In fact we must dissociate ourselves from this doctrine of essences, not only because with it substantial forms again loom up, but also because such a doctrine invariably involves the hypostatizing of universals. This in turn breeds a tendency to transmogrify the universal considered simply in its own right into something all-important and fundamental. And behind this tendency there always lurks, consciously or unconsciously, the postulate of deductivity: "Derivation" is possible only from universal statements, and these, therefore, appear to be an expression of the very principles of being.

Behind all this there hides more than one mistake. Although it is very true that all principles are universal, it does not follow that all universals are principles. There is also a very peripheral universal—for instance in the recurrent external characteristics revealed by widely scattered particulars—and it is precisely this universal which first offers itself to experience. But any attempt to classify things or animate beings according to such universals would furnish a classificatory order, but one which would completely miss the ontic condition of things. General traits of external appearance, arbitrarily gathered, do not indicate where the principles of being lie. For that we need other criteria. One of the weaknesses of the old ontology consisted in its failure to provide these criteria.

To this is added a second weakness. Even though it is unassailably true that only from universal statements may something be derived (deduced), yet it does not follow that universal statements from which something is derived express something "ontically" universal. But if they do not, they are untrue statements—in Kantian language, synthetic judgments a priori without "objective validity." Of course, deductions can be logically drawn from such statements just as well as from true ones. But the conclusions will be just as little true as the premises. No philosophical aspiration, however moderate its claims, is thereby served.

Evidently it is this very mistake that the central argument of the *Critique of Pure Reason* combats. It does so by countering all such deductivity—one might say, the ontological deduction—with a "transcendental deduction" that concerns itself with the objective validity of those a priori principles by virtue of which synthetic judgments are a priori true. It is well known how much store Kant set by this deduction. But considering that it rests completely on categories tied up with experience (for this deduction confined the objective validity of the categories to "possible experience"), it is readily realized that it precludes *a limine* a purely a priori knowledge of the essence of things. This achievement of the *Critique* is at first a negative one. But its results are thoroughly affirmative and, as such, are of the greatest importance.

All ontology has to do with fundamental assertions about being as such. Assertions of this sort are precisely what we call categories of being. Like the Kantian categories—which, as far as content is concerned, are also precisely this: fundamental assertions about being—they have the character of universal constitutive principles comprising all more specialized ontological assertions. Hence, the new ontology might be expected to provide a transcendental deduction also of these ontological assertions. Otherwise, it is argued, it could not guarantee their objective validity. That, however, would mean that this ontology in its turn was in need of an epistemological foundation which would have to provide the justification of a priori principles of an even wider scope.

Thereby a way for ontology is traced, and this way once more follows the scheme of the old deductivity. But it is here that the roads of the old and the new ontology part. Just as in regard to the problem of being it is today no longer a question of substantial forms and of the teleological determination of actual processes by these forms, so also the problem at issue is no longer that of a *post factum* justification of a priori principles. The categories with which the new ontology deals are won neither by a definition of the universal nor through derivation from a formal table of judgments. They are rather gleaned step by step from an observation of existing realities. And since, of course, this method of their discovery does not allow for an absolute criterion of truth, here no more than in any other field of knowledge, it must be added that the procedure of finding and rechecking is a laborious and cumbersome one. Under the limited conditions of human research it requires manifold detours, demands constant corrections, and, like all genuine scholarly work, never comes to an end.

Here one may truly and literally speak of new ways of ontology. The basic thesis can possibly be formulated like this: The categories of being are not a priori principles. Only such things as insights, cognitions, and judgments can be a priori. In fact the whole contrast between a priori and a posteriori is only an epistemological one. But ontology is not concerned with knowledge, much less with mere judgments, but with the object of knowledge in so far as this object is at the same time "transobjective," that is, independent of whether or to what extent being is actually transformed into an object of knowledge. The principles of the object in its very being are in no way *eo ipso* also cognitive principles. In some fields they can be quite heterogeneous, as the manifold admixtures of the unknowable in nearly all basic problems of philosophy amply prove. From this alone it follows that the principles of being cannot be a priori principles of our intellect, that they, as a matter of fact, are just as indifferent to the dividing line between the knowable and the unknowable as the being whose principles they are.

At this point it is incumbent upon us radically to unlearn the old and start to learn the new, not only if our approach be from the old ontology, but also if it be from the standpoint of transcendental epistemology. Of course, as far as their content goes, ontological categories can occasionally coincide with cognitive categories; and within certain limits this must be the case wherever an objectively valid knowledge of objects takes place a priori. But it must not be supposed that this occurs everywhere and without limits. The apriorism in our knowledge is subject to a very fundamental limitation, because our categories of understanding coincide at best only in part with the principles of being. This coincidence reaches farthest where it is a question of insights that are practically relevant and indispensable to the business of life—in other words, in that field of objects to which our understanding is best suited. And correspondingly, it fails most signally where we are confronted with broad theoretical questions concerning our total world picture and its philosophical interpretation. For it is manifest that with our rational principles we can grasp a priori only that aspect of the real world which in itself is framed in accordance with those same principles.

One further step must here be taken. The statement that ontological categories are not a priori principles means simply that they cannot be immediately recognized a priori. Inasmuch as they are at all accessible to knowledge, they must be grasped by other methods. For this, a point of departure seems to offer itself in the relation between cognitive and ontological categories. We already know why this relation must involve at least a partial identity. It might then be concluded: In so far as the ontological categories are the same as the cognitive categories, it should be possible to discover the former as included in the latter. In this way one might at least be able to grasp a priori a sector of the ontological principles.

Even this hope proves deceptive. In the first place, we have no criterion to measure the extent of that categorial identity. And precisely where on practical grounds we are more or less certain of this identity—in everyday life and for our natural orientation in the world—this identity is philosophically worthless because it does not bear upon the problems of philosophy. But where these begin, it becomes extraordinarily questionable and soon fails us completely. In the second place, in our cognitive apparatus there is lacking one fundamental prerequisite for so exploiting this identity: an immediate knowledge of our own cognitive categories.

It lies in the nature of all knowledge to be directed not toward itself but toward its object. What, in the process of knowing, the knower becomes conscious of are traits of the object only, not traits of his own action. Least of all do the inner conditions of his action fall within his consciousness; but cognitive categories are counted among these. So, philosophy had to pass through a long historical process before it finally began to become aware of a few of the cognitive categories as such. This awareness requires a reversal of the natural cognitive direction, a turning around, as it were, from the object to the knower. And in fact with this reversal, knowledge of a second order sets in where knowledge itself is made the object of knowledge. This epistemological reflection is "secondary" and must be carried through "against" the natural attitude. When it sets in, it does not lead immediately to the categories of understanding but by a special method must be directed toward them.

This is why not only the ontological categories but even our own cognitive categories on which all knowledge a priori rests are not themselves known a priori. In fact, it must be added that generally they remain unknown in the knowledge of the object. They function in our knowledge but do not in turn become an object of knowledge. Only through the intervention of epistemological reflection are they brought to the light of consciousness. But that is a phase of knowledge reached only late in the historical process. Were the functioning of these categories in our knowledge dependent upon our knowledge of them, all human knowledge, even the most naïve, would have to await a philosophy to make them conscious. But since philosophy actually presupposes naïve knowledge, philosophy, on this hypothesis, could never have arrived at the simple understanding of objects.

Actually, the reverse order prevails: Although cognitive categories are the first condition of our knowledge—especially of the a priori elements in it, which are nowhere absent, not even in the naïve world view—they are not the first to be recognized in it. They are not unknowable, but can be known only indirectly, namely as mediated through the simple knowledge of the objects which is based upon their functioning. If they are known at all, they are, we might say, rather the thing known last. And this order is irreversible. That explains why they are hardest to know. The many detours and blind alleys by which epistemology tries to arrive at them provide an unambiguous demonstration of this fact.

Thus the possibility of making ontological categories comprehensible by a detour through the cognitive categories must be considered altogether negligible. One might believe that in the last analysis it is rather the cognitive categories which can be made intelligible by a detour through the ontological categories. The latter, at any rate, lie in the natural direction of cognition—in the background of objects—albeit the simple knowledge of objects may not penetrate to them. But since all knowledge of objects has in it the tendency toward progressive advance, it may very well, by dint of a progressive deepening, lead directly to ontological categories.

That this is so, at least in principle, is demonstrated by the most ancient and primitive form of philosophical research, which, long before the appearance of epistemological thought, sought single-mindedly after the principles of being. An out-standing example of such a search is furnished by the whole sequence of the great pre-Socratics. And it cannot be denied that in this effort they really found various ontological prin-ciples which, in the course of a much later and critically ma-ture exploration, have proved valid.

There is, however, no need of harking back this far. Where, after all, did Kant take his categories from? Certainly not from the Table of Judgments which, it must be remembered, he first had to complete for this purpose. The truth of the mat-ter comes out rather in the Analysis of Principles: The cate-gories are drawn from the content of knowledge such as it has emerged from the whole field of scientific research. That, however, means that they are drawn from our knowledge of objects; in other words, they are taken from the object itself in so far as it has disclosed itself at a certain stage of scientific knowledge. This is revealed most clearly in the Analogies of Experience. From the analysis of process and change arises the category of substance; and from the analysis of objectively determined succession the existence of a causal relationship is made intelligible. Of course, to the idealistically trained think-er it will by no means be apparent that by proceeding in this manner we arrive directly only at categories of the object and not at all at "pure concepts of the understanding" (nor at fundamental principles of the Determining Judgment). It is all the more noticeable, however, to the latter-day interpreter who takes the trouble of re-enacting in his own thought and critically illuminating the Kantian conclusions.

After this we need hardly waste words in showing that much the same must hold even to a higher degree of Fichte's and Schelling's attempts to derive their categories from one single principle. Critics have often remarked that actually everything is here taken from experience while it is ascribed to the Ego, to subconscious intelligence, or to reason. In this form the objection is certainly too coarse. The fact is, however, that behind all those apparent derivations there hides a detailed knowledge of the world of objects—a knowledge that makes itself felt throughout and provides the entire content.

All this yields a fundamental lesson: In so far as we can gain any knowledge at all of categories, we do not gain it by a priori methods nor by raising principles of reason into consciousness, but rather through an analysis of objects to the extent that they are intelligible to us. In this way, however, we grasp in the first place ontological categories only, not cognitive categories as such. The latter are arrived at only through reflection on the cognitive function by proceeding backwards from the comprehended ontological categories.

This state of affairs is of the greatest import. First, it follows that epistemology, in regard to the problem of categories, is not independent but presupposes an ontological understanding of the whole field of the objects of knowledge. Moreover, it follows that epistemology, taken by itself, cannot be a fundamental philosophy as the transcendental mode of argument has always tacitly assumed. Rather it itself needs an ontological foundation. Second, in view of this order of dependency, the question can now be answered concerning the proper way of philosophy, if it is to comprehend ontological categories.

This question, before all others, becomes acute once it is understood that the way leading to the goal is neither a purely a priori one nor one of "transcendental reflection" (upon cognitive conditions). It may also be assumed as a well-known fact that a purely empiricist path is even less promising. All the same, the way with which we are concerned is not an enigmatic one. Indeed, it is historically well known, and it is followed wherever ontological categories are discovered by inference. It is the old and tried way of analysis—a method familiar to the ancients and one which in modern times, since Descartes, has become the prevalent procedure of philosophical inquiry.

The way of the new ontology, then, presents itself as a categorial analysis—a procedure exhausted neither by induction nor by deduction, consisting neither in a purely a posteriori knowledge nor in a purely a priori knowledge. It presupposes the whole breadth of experience, that of everyday life and practical existence as well as that of science. It even presupposes philosophical experience recorded in the historical course of human thought as a long series of attempts, failures, and self-corrections. This whole sum of accumulated experience furnishes the starting level of actual data. To this sum of experience must be reckoned also the elements of a critical insight into its own uncertainty factors—in a sense its most important ingredient.

This starting level, then, is not simply the naïve consciousness of the world as phenomenology has tried to understand it. That would be a consciousness far too poor in content. It has also long since become evident that it is never to be grasped as such free of interpretation. For it is not the consciousness of the one who philosophizes, and from his actual standpoint it can at best be reached by a regressive conclusion. This regressive mode of concluding about a naïve consciousness—the consciousness of the child, for example—is, however, subject to such manifold deceptions that its results become highly questionable as a starting level. Everything depends on what is given; what is reached by conclusion, however, is precisely not given.

Only that may be considered given which the philosophizing consciousness is already endowed with the moment it starts its analysis. The sorting out of the certain from the doubtful is already a matter of philosophical effort. It was an error to exclude the scientific findings. True, the sciences interpret their material, but at the same time they open a view toward a multitude of new fields of content. These also belong to the starting level of analysis. They should not be isolated and established as the sole field of orientation, as was done in neo-Kantianism. But they must not be neglected either.

The analysis itself, then, is a procedure of purely regressive conclusion with respect to the content. It rests upon the conviction that the ontological principles must somehow be included in being and that, consequently, it must be possible to discover them if only a sufficiently broad basis of ontic data is supplied. For naturally they do not lie exposed to view in the data as such but must be made visible by a penetrating study. What can be found by this method necessarily goes beyond the given, so far as content is concerned, if for no other reason than because of its claim to higher universality. For the same reason it is never free of a certain element of the hypothetical. But this can be considerably lessened if afterwards the result is verified by means of a broader material of data. Accordingly, the history of the discovery of the ontological categories (a history which for many categories can be traced from the earliest thinkers down to those of our time) shows clearly how an ever renewed criticism improves progressively upon hypothetical conclusions. Only at a late date is a certain stabilization of single ontological categories attained, and even today the formulation of most of them is still in process.

In this manner the categorial analysis reveals itself as a science which, in spite of its very early beginnings, is still in the cocoon stage of its development. In the last century, which was predominantly interested in epistemological questions, it made little progress and thus today is still lagging behind other branches of knowledge. How far it will be able to catch up only the future can show.

It is worth noticing here that ontology with this type of procedure again approaches the methods of many special sciences from which, once in the days of the "realism of universals," it had mistakenly separated itself. It was positive science which first developed and critically illuminated the analytic method along with the hypothetical element which it involves. However, positive science is unable to apply the method to the ultimate fundamental problems. That falls to the lot of philosophy. And by its application in philosophy this procedure will become intensified, thereby revealing the full measure of its fruitfulness.

Chapter III

A New Concept of Reality

WITH the preceding disquisition the speculative metaphysical component of the old ontology is radically discarded. The ontological problem is limited to less ambitious problems readily surveyed and expressible in a language devoid of sentimental overtones. But this limitation is directed only against a thinking which is given to the mere fanciful construction of a *Weltanschauung,* and to the conjuring up of a transcendent world beyond the boundaries of experience, not, however, against the problems of the psychic or spiritual life or even less against those inescapable questions of meaning and value which stir in the human mind.

If from our point of view one looks, for example, at the metaphysics of the spirit and of freedom as expounded by Fichte and Hegel, the new ontology would only limit their theses but would by no means basically reject them. It cannot justify the contention that being in its entirety rests upon the Ego (albeit an absolute one) or on the spirit. But in no way will it deny that the spirit, where it really appears, has freedom and activity—and, in fact, of such a sort that it extends over the whole expanse of being and has a far-reaching power to transform it. Indeed, it may rather be expected that the new ontology will discover a new meaning in the problem of the power and freedom of the spirit by seeking to determine the being of the spirit and its activity in relation to the being of the rest of the world.

That would have been difficult for the old ontology. It was fundamentally oriented toward the being of material things and, in addition, toward the organism. It interpreted psychic life organologically, and it assigned the spirit to the kingdom of essences. Therefore it could not place the spirit within the world of reality. Its reality seemed to be of an altogether different type from that of things, a timeless being without change or individuality. However, the new ontology is distinguished from the old in that it removes all such limitations. It starts from the level of the given upon which it bases itself, and which embraces psychic and spiritual being just as much as the being of nature. For the spirit does not stand outside the world of reality. It belongs completely to it, has the same temporality, the same coming into being and passing away as material things and living beings. In short, it has the same reality. For this reason alone can it have an effect in this world and experience the effects of the world upon it, have its own fate and its own field of action within this world.

Against such a view, however, there arises a series of very old prejudices, rendered almost venerable through tradition. The mode of being of material things cannot be the same as that of thoughts, acts, mental conditions, or insights, can it? Is it not precisely here, straight through the middle of the world and of man himself, that there goes the great dividing line which Descartes drew with his doctrine of two substances: on the one side the spatially extended, the extensive, the measurable, the mechanical; on the other side the nonspatial, the nonextended inner world which never mixes with the outer world?

In this dichotomy the true and the untrue are disastrously confused. It is true that spatiality and materiality separate the two worlds of being from each other, but the idea of man as an entity composed of two heterogeneous substances has shown itself to be erroneous. The human being as a whole is too much of an indivisible unity. His activity, passivity, and general condition are too obviously both corporeal and psychic. And, above all, the very life of man consists of an inseparable merging of the inner and the outer. Only an imaginative belief in immortality can derive benefit from this separation of substances. The real concrete life, with its constant blending of the two spheres, is not to be understood in this manner.

The basic mistake in this view is that reality is confused with materiality. Hence reality is believed to be limited to the spatial. But then human destinies as well as historical conditions and occurrence would not be real. Precisely that would be made unreal which in life carries the heaviest-felt weight of reality. That, of course, is out of the question. The whole view rests on a much too narrow and obviously ill-constructed concept of reality, a concept twisted to fit a certain *Weltanschauung*. This *Weltanschauung*, however, which here inadvertently enters into play, must needs be a basically materialistic one. That is reason enough to reconsider the matter, especially if we are seriously concerned about the being of the spirit and its historical forms.

The true characteristics of reality do not depend on the categories of space and matter but on those of time and individuality. Ontologically considered, time and space are not categories of equal worth: Time is by far more fundamental than space. Only material things and living beings, including the processes through which their existence flows, are spatial. But spiritual and psychic processes, as well as material processes, are temporal. For everything real is in time and only a part of it in space—we might say, only one half of the real world, its lower forms.

Inseparably joined with temporality is individuality. This consists in nothing but singleness and uniqueness. The real is perishable and thereby also unrepeatable. The same *sort* of thing recurs, never the same identical thing. This holds true of historical events as well as of cosmic motions, of persons as well as of things. Only the universal recurs, for, considered by itself, it is timeless, always existing, eternal. This timelessness was once considered in the old ontology to be a being of a higher order, indeed, even the only true being. But, in truth, it is rather a dependent, a merely ideal being, and the universal has reality nowhere else but in the real particulars which are both temporal and individual. What once was considered a kingdom of perfection, the kingdom of essences, whose faint copies things were supposed to be, has proved itself to be a kingdom of incomplete being which becomes independent only through abstraction. In the recognition of this lies perhaps the most striking contrast of the new ontology to the old.

That is why the new ontology can very well grapple with the deep problems of German idealism, why it can deal with the spirit and freedom, social life and history, just as well as with the cosmos and the organism. Hence new light may be expected to be shed by it on the characteristic situation and activity of man as a spiritual being within a non-spiritual, law-determined world.

These reflections are but a small section from a chapter on categorial analysis. Here they are only sketched. They justly demand a much more exact discussion of space, time, process, psychic act, reality, and so forth. Particularly reality, the pure mode of being of the structures and processes which form the world, is a very difficult subject for analysis. In order to understand reality the philosopher must start with an examination of the relationship of possibility and actuality—for centuries the fundamental problem of ontology. And the revolution in the whole problem of being extends even to these very foundations of being. For what the old ontology teaches about potency and act—a relationship according to which everything real is a realization of a pre-existing disposition and all being is destined to become what it is by disposition—proves to be far from adequate in view of the broadened problem of reality. It is incumbent upon us to introduce a new concept of "real possibility" (*Realmöglichkeit*) which no longer coincides with essential possibility but which signifies the totality of conditions present at a given time within the real context. To this must correspond just as novel a concept of "actual reality" (*Realwirklichkeit*) which is no longer thought of as the goal of an anthropomorphically conceived tendency, as if the processes in the cosmos were tied to the activity of an intelligence. Rather such actual reality must in every case be considered to be the complex result of a far-flung context of determinants. A whole science concerns itself with these inner relationships of reality considered as a mode of being. It forms the core of the new ontology, and, in contrast to an analysis of categories directed toward the structural content, it may be called "modal analysis."

Meanwhile, it may be necessary to start even farther back. For the traditional prejudices against the problem of being reach still further. Today many analysts, moved though they are by a genuine philosophical impetus, have a deep-seated aversion to every form of inquiry which gives precedence to the problem of being. By being they mean something rigid, motionless, and even inimicable to life, something which hampers man in his activity, depriving him of his independence and freedom. Activism in the Fichtian fashion, which makes the world dependent on man and sets activity above everything stationary, is the ideal which guides them. They think that only thus can justice be done to the essence of man.

However much we may sympathize with the underlying practical attitude, the manner in which these philosophers hope to reach their goal is completely wrong. So they cannot carry through what in tendency is wholly justified. Their presuppositions do not ring true. In the real world we are confronted with no rigid system, not even with a world "finished" in every respect, which is simply to be taken as a fact and in which there remains nothing for us to do. It is an old error to think that being is the opposite of motion and becoming. Once in the beginnings of philosophy this opposition was set up by the Eleatics. Though much combated, something of it survived in certain reactionary views of nineteenth-century thought. Today it leads an underground existence in the thinking of those who have not learned from the history of philosophy.

Becoming is no opposite of being but is a form of being. Everything real is in flux, involved in a constant coming into, or going out of, existence. Motion and becoming form the universal mode of being of the real, no matter whether it be a question of material things, living forms, or human beings. Rest and rigidity are only found in the ideal essences of the old ontology. And if it is the first task of the new ontology to define the mode of being of the real, this means especially that we must define the mode of being that characterizes becoming. This task in itself is manifold because according to the rungs or strata of the real, becoming takes on different forms. Thus the condition of being alive—understood as the complex life process of the organic—differs from the simple spatial-physical motion and, likewise, the psychic process from the organic, the spiritual-historical from the psychic. But all have the same mode of being, reality; they are all real occurrences, real life, and so forth. The problem of being, then, is not concerned with an imagined world of immobility but rather with the Being of Becoming.

Here is a simple example which should not require many words. Motion which is not being could not be real motion. To deal with it would be idle. But the same goes for real life, real volition, real action, real decision, and real initiative. There is no sense in concealing from oneself the fact that everywhere, in human life as well as in the transmutation of energy in the economy of nature, this "being real" is a mode of being without which the phenomena of the world would be without import or meaning. It is precisely with this factor that ontology must deal. In life it might seem to us self-evident. But philosophy begins by discovering the uncomprehended and enigmatic in the self-evident.

Aside from this, the rest of the world cannot be neglected for the sake of man and his activity. For, after all, man is placed in the midst of it, and is dependent upon it in incalculably many ways. Extreme activism does not wish to hear anything of this dependence. It suspects behind it a universal determinism which would enslave all spontaneity and freedom. It is its privilege to reject this. But its prejudice consists in assuming that dependence in a certain respect already offers a menace to human freedom. Freedom without dependence is the unlimited freedom of caprice. An activity without trammel and resistance would be an effortless game without a struggle and without the risk of engagement.

This Fichte saw and formulated very exactly: Through the resistance of something pre-existent—"a world upon which I act"—the Ego first grows really active. It could be added: All activity must search for the means of realizing its purposes.

But activity itself does not bring forth the means; it chooses them. Choice, however, is possible only in an existing world which proffers a veritable manifold.

Finally, no one can possibly believe that everything in life depends on man alone. Like the "magic idealist" Novalis, he would then have to believe that it depended only upon him to lift the magic wand and to create for himself a world such as he desired it. This is a poetic daydream. In any case the power of man does not reach that far. Whoever in a metaphysics of man would maintain this would miss the real essence of man; even Fichte was far from committing this error. The uniqueness of the position of man in the world of reality consists precisely in that there is a certain margin for his will. But by no means is everything subject to his will. In order to carry through his plans in the world, he must learn to know and understand it. He will rule it within the ambit of his purposes and interests only in so far as he obeys its laws. That is the secret of all technical skill, all domination of nature, but also of the ruling and guidance of the human being itself. For this being, too, has its own unique autonomous determination, and only within the limits set by this autonomy can it be transformed. The same goes for social life, by far man's widest field of activity: here through his organizing activity there emerge conditions, difficulties, and needs which he neither desired nor foresaw but with which hereafter he must come to terms. And it is this necessity which first brings into play the activity of his faculties, the creative seeking and finding of remedies, foresight, and the strength of daring.

Freedom, too, is possible only in a world which, with its determination, provides it with a foil as well as an obstacle. He who closes his eyes to the world as it is closes them also to the essence of his own activity and power. For no omnipotence is given to the spirit but only a limited power. Just as limited is man's freedom, tied everywhere to conditions of realization which he did not create but which leave him an opening for his own initiative. To descry this opening in the midst of the manifold limitations of the existing determinacy of being is the work of a spontaneous, spiritual insight, and it demands the unrelenting effort of the intellectual powers in the life and learning of the individual as well as in the historical development of cumulative experiences, discoveries, and inventions.

The real task of philosophy concerning the problem of freedom consists fundamentally in properly defining the limits of freedom. It must be understood as a freedom conditioned by manifold dependencies and maintaining itself against them. Otherwise philosophy would be dealing only with the mere dream of freedom, not with its reality. It would then be dealing with neither the real spirit nor the real man.

Chapter IV

The New Ontology
and the New Anthropology

CLOSELY related to the prejudice which has just been rejected is a doctrine which continued to dominate both neo-Kantianism and the so-called life-philosophy. It has to do with the relation of organic life to spiritual life. The autonomy of the spiritual life had been grasped and had been brought to definition in certain of its fundamental traits, and now it was believed that all dependence of the spirit upon the processes of corporeal life should be denied. This was at variance with a multitude of facts well known in medical science. Physiology and psychology, the latter at that time mostly following the trend of natural science, raised loud objections. Nevertheless, the thesis once posited, philosophers continued to cling to it, because they were at a loss how to reconcile with such dependence the autonomy of the spirit, discovered after long struggles.

In this line of thought there arose a concept of "understanding" (*Verstehen*) which apparently outranked all cognitive comprehension. This concept was determined by the working method of the so-called "sciences of the spirit"

(*Geisteswissenschaft*), primarily the science of history. Historical deeds and events have to be made intelligible through their inner significance, their meaning. This concept of meaning was stretched so as to include any and everything that needed to be understood from within itself. Comprehension, so it was now thought, is directed toward the external; understanding, toward meaning. Material nature is comprehensible only: It has no "within." The old doctrine of purposes is unmistakably hidden in this concept of meaning. For the interpretation of human actions it is undoubtedly justified: Actions are purposive activities. But are events in the context of the world of the same nature? Is it permissible to approach them with the demands inherent in the concept of understanding? Is it true even for historical events that they are everywhere tending toward a meaning, or does not also the meaningless play a part in the course of history? And is not human endeavor in history just the unabating struggle against the meaningless?

Obviously a metaphysical prejudgment is involved in this doctrine of meaning and the understanding of meaning. Not everything in the world of reality, perhaps only the least part of it, is meaningful; nor is understanding the adequate means of comprehension for all types of objects. A "within," however, can very well be found also in that which is not directed toward purposes, such as the movement of masses in cosmic space. It may consist, for instance, in the fact that an object is determined by laws, or in the form of its determinateness, or in its being a multiplicity bound together into unity, or in the balance of concord and discord. It is no mere accident that nothing but fundamental ontological categories impose themselves upon us when we wish to express the inner essence of natural structures. For the categories of being actually form, in a very definite and tenable sense, a "within of things."

The method which leads to this "within" is still that same method which was once characterized by Kant as the method of "observation and analysis." In the case of the most general questions of principle, this is the method of categorial analysis.

Much more important than this reflection is the fact that the activity of man, spiritual life and historical actuality, can by no means be adequately grasped by an understanding of meaning. With this concept we are still in the air, with no firm ground under our feet. We shall have to return to comprehension based upon the knowledge of laws. For the firm ground on which the spirit rests is not itself spirit, nor even anything of its kind, but is just what is opposite and foreign to it, the wide realm of nature, in the first place organic nature, but indirectly also inorganic nature.

On this point idealism did not stand the test, nor did the idealism of life-philosophy, even though it had been cleansed of all heaven-storming metaphysics and had become very sober. It too still shared the old view of a spiritual life based upon itself—as if somewhere in the world there was a floating spirit without the foundation of corporeal life adjusted to the total structure of the world of reality. Practical life tells quite another story—the same story which all positive sciences tell in so far as they treat of man: There is no such thing as a floating spirit. All true spirit is supported—supported by nothing less than the whole hierarchical order of the world down to material reality.

Without doubt man is a spiritual being. This constitutes his superiority over other living things. But he is not solely a spiritual being. He cannot disregard the spatial conditions in which he lives. To be sure, he can do so in thought, but he cannot really—that is, in living and acting—be where he is not. He can, of course, go there, but only *in corpore*. The spirit is, and remains, bound to the body. It exists only in organic being, rests on its life, and lives from its energies. And as organic life belongs to the material world and remains integrated into its transmutation of energy, it is also directly supported by it.

At this point the new ontology finds itself confronted with a very serious task. If man—even as a spiritual being—cannot be understood without the world within which he finds himself, it is necessary to understand him in terms of his connection with the total world-structure. Indeed, it is necessary to define his essence anew from this point of view. In the old ontology the opposite tendency was present, to see the whole world as relative to man, to view all forms and relationships in the hierarchy of the world as ordered toward him, as though he constituted the final purpose of the world order. A very different picture presents itself if one starts from the real wonders of organic life, from the genetic connection of morphologically cognate beings, and from the thorough adaptation of the organic functions to the conditions of the surrounding world. There the opposite appears: The world is not ordered toward man, but he is ordered toward the world. Everything in him is relative to the world and can be understood as an adaptation to the general all-comprehensive situation in which he must survive.

Once one has advanced so far, it is necessary to go still further with this reflection. Man, aside from all adaptation, is conditioned to the highest degree by the whole hierarchy of real forms. His being in the world presupposes the being of the world. Without it he cannot live. The world, on the other hand, can very well exist without him. The organic world—considered not just with respect to its individual parts but taken as a whole—is a presupposition of his existence. And since, in the same manner, the organic world has the inorganic one for its presupposition, it must further be asserted that all of nature from the bottom up to the living beings akin to man is a condition of his existence.

Obviously this relationship cannot be reversed. Hence we arrive at the simple insight that man as such is a late phenomenon in the genetic order of the forms which constitute the world. About his genesis itself nothing is thereby settled in advance. It remains problematic in some respects, and in no way is it necessary that ontology concern itself with this problem. Essential for ontology is the principle involved, that here is an irreversible conditional relationship. The lower tiers of being are independent of the higher ones and do not need them, but the higher are dependent on the lower.

No hasty conclusions should here be drawn. All this has nothing to do with materialism. The dependency in question does not imply that all organic life is to be explained in terms of physical material relations, or all psychic and spiritual life in terms of organic conditions. How far the dependence "on that below" reaches, what it covers, how much and what can be explained by it—all this is quite another question. Such a dependency in no way excludes autonomy. Meanwhile it must only be granted that the *conditio sine qua non* of the higher forms of being is always provided by the lower forms and, in the last analysis, by the entire series of the lower forms.

In this respect the new doctrine of man that has become current in our time is really of pioneering significance, in so far as it makes people aware of the far-reaching determination of a national spiritual life by inheritance factors. It may well be that the phenomena of race differences impress us today as being only vaguely defined in many respects, and that the hopes of people with a biological bias to solve cultural problems on this basis are exaggerated. But there is no doubt about the division of human kind into races of very definite and relatively constant hereditary types with characteristic abilities and tendencies. The central fact in all this is the corporeal-psychic unity of man. For there are not two different inheritance factors but only one which, despite all the variety and seeming independence of bodily and psychic peculiarities, nevertheless shows unmistakably the wholeness of a single, integrated type.

Therewith biology is confronted with tasks which at this time it is in no position to tackle. What would here have to be ascertained does not merely concern the bare fact of inherited characteristics but their inner laws, the causes and boundaries of their stability, the scope of their variability, their malleability and transformability as well as their relation to the enormous number of external factors continually operating upon them. No one can deny that the latter play an incalculable part in the psychic field. But it would be important to find a basis for determining how far into spiritual life the biologically comprehensible elements of inheritance reach and which of its aspects they influence.

In order to attack these tasks biology would first have to gain sufficient insight into the purely organic process of inheritance. But this prerequisite is still far from being fulfilled. The visible carriers of inherited characteristics in the germ cells are known, but only in their general aspect, not in the details of their structures. And even if these, too, could be ascertained microscopically we would still know nothing of the ways they operate in their function of determining forms. For their determining function stands in a unique reciprocal relation to a confusing multitude of other functions. Among these the influence exercised by the total situation is probably the most important factor, although it varies in the evolutionary process from stage to stage.

The difficulty lies by no means only in the small size of the structure nor in the unapproachability of the component processes. It also lies in something of fundamental importance: in the interpenetration of very different modes of determination. In so far as the total process of the organic development is determined by elements of the system of hereditary dispositions, its determination is a prospective self-directing one. In so far as it depends on the variable function of the total situation, it is a causal one. Of these two forms of determination it is only the latter which we know with precision. For it is present in all processes of reality, and it is the sole ruler in the world of inanimate nature. The former, on the other hand, which constitutes the unique organological character of the development of the organism (and, therewith, the factor determining the reproduction of the specific form), is only known by its effect. Its inner mode of functioning, the categorial structure of the determination itself, is absolutely unknown and may be regarded as impenetrable to our present methods of investigation.

There are many such unknowable factors in the processual structure of organic life. The assimilating and constructive function in the metabolism, for example, the so-called assimilation of matter received, is of the same puzzling nature. And in both cases it is just the eminently formative (morphogenetic) factor in the total process on which this irrationality depends. It is no different with the regulative and recuperative phenomena of living beings nor, in fact, with the phenomena, obvious to everyone, of adaptation and purposiveness.

The further we penetrate into these problems, the more the riddles deepen. Naturally we will ask why this is so. The answer can be found when we consider the unique situation of man who has the organic world both outside himself and within. He himself is a living being. But in that segment of the world to which he has access he also meets the organism as an object. Indeed, even his own body is given to him in a twofold manner. It is felt by him in subjective immediacy as his own body with its varying conditions. At the same time it is a visible and touchable object like other spatial-material objects.

On closer inspection neither of the two types of data is found to get at the specifically organic life itself. The external datum, though presenting itself as an object, offers no more than an appearance. The inner datum, on the other hand, is subjective, undifferentiated, and vague. Neither affords an approach to organic function. Only science feels its way toward the heart of the matter by chiefly leaning on the objective view. But it advances slowly with short steps, and in regard to fundamental questions it must make use of many hypotheses.

The fact is that our cognitive equipment has no organ of its own for the comprehension of life as such. It has a highly developed organ for the understanding of material objects. Hence an exact scientific knowledge is here possible. Within certain limits it has also an organ for its own psychic inwardness. Therefore there is, at any rate, an immediate certainty of inner processes, and psychology makes use of this. But there is no similar approach to organic life. We can only probe into it from the adjacent strata of being, from the lower stratum as well as from the higher one, from inorganic reality as well as from psychic reality.

However, both of these detours involve the introduction of areas of being as mediating devices, and through the use of categories drawn from these areas, an attempt is made to understand organic being. The objective view tends to interpret everything in the manner of the exact sciences; the subjective view, in the manner of psychic life. The former uses for its interpretation the determination schema of causal relationship; the latter, that of teleological relationship. Therefore a mechanistic interpretation of organic functions still exists today side by side with a teleological interpretation, and, correspondingly, there are two camps of philosophical theories of organic life. On both sides the fact is overlooked that the organism has its own peculiar form of determination. And that is the above-suggested determination of a formative process by a system of dispositions. We are here in the unique situation of being obliged not only to assume hypothetically this kind of determination but of finding it unmistakably and forcibly thrust upon us throughout the whole area of the study of animate nature, even though we are unable to detect its categorial structure.

We must have this situation before us if we wish to give an account of how the question of the inheritability of intellectual dispositions stands. For the time being, science can only accept the fact of this inheritability empirically but cannot see through it with exact methods. Ontologically decisive, however, is not how much a science at a certain stage can explain, but exclusively what must be accepted and taken into account on the basis of the phenomena. The limits of knowability are not the limits of being.

This point of view is decisive for categorial analysis. It must search for its categories just where empirical science has gaps —not, of course, with the ambition of developing them into definitions through bold assumptions but with the opposite tendency of recognizing their irrationality and deliberately integrating it into the total picture. Perhaps there are no ontological categories without an irrational component. Even the well-known principles of substantiality and causality are, in their essence, not wholly knowable. What substance actually is, how it maintains itself through its incessant transformation, how a cause goes about producing an effect—all these things cannot be explained any further. Nevertheless a great number of phenomena can be explained on the basis of these categories. And so it is, also, with the unique organic determination by a system of dispositions: By far not everything in it can be reduced to comprehensible data. But all the same, certain basic phenomena of organic life can be derived from it. To these phenomena belong the hereditary constancy of organic properties in the passage of generations and with it also the constancy of psychic and intellectual dispositions.

The older theories of the spirit all shied away from incorporating non-spiritual factors into the structure of the spiritual world. They feared thereby to fall a prey to materialism. But there is no cause for this apprehension, provided the mistake is not made of setting up a radical either-or, as if by admitting certain organic components everything in the realm of the spirit becomes at once dependent on the organism. Non-spiritual factors of highly divergent types may very well enter without the spiritual life losing its uniqueness and characteristic independence. For all spirit rests on the broader cosmic context and depends upon it. It must, therefore, include, and be subject to, the manifold threads of determination, not created by it, which form the cosmic context. But that does not prevent it from having its own self-determination and from confronting the powers of lower nature with a very definite independence.

The new anthropology rediscovers these relationships. It has room for the autonomy of spiritual life but knows, also, how to unite with it the organic stratum of the human being. That is possible only on the basis of certain ontological ideas. The absolute self-sufficiency of the spirit as defended by idealist theories cannot then be maintained. But the autonomy of the spirit does not depend on doctrines of this type which are at variance with the phenomena. All independence of the spirit which we know is independence in dependence, and the dependence is a weighty and many-sided one. To dispute this dependence would be closing one's eyes to the facts. But a reconciliation of dependence with independence can be accomplished only by an ontological clarification of the basic relationship between the heterogeneous strata of reality.

Chapter | V

The Stratified Structure of the World

AS THE preceding argument shows, the purposes of anthropology, aside from everything else, demand a new ontology. For an anthropology rests on a philosophy of the organic as its presupposition. The latter, however, cannot be constructed without a general ontology. It is an element in the system of sciences, just as its object, the organism, is an element in the structure of the world.

So in order to reach decisive conclusions here, a total view of the world structure is needed. The basis for it is available once it has been shown that the same mode of being, reality, encompasses everything from matter to the spirit. What is left to be done, the development of both the multiplicity of forms of being and the interpenetration of dependence and independence, is a matter of categorial analysis.

This multiplicity of forms obviously constitutes a ladder whose order of rungs in general is well known: inanimate object, plant, animal, man, society, and perhaps a few others. History might be added as that which embraces the national communities as they coexist with each other and distinguish themselves from each other. On closer examination it is found that each of these rungs of being includes, in its turn, a whole ladder. This is best known with reference to the plant and animal kingdoms. But it can be seen to hold good for inorganic nature, too, when, following the order of magnitude, the dynamic structure is traced from the atom to the cosmic system. More hidden and, as it were, more irregular is the gradation in regard to man and to forms of society. But, of course, it is not lacking there either.

If one were content to lay down this hierarchy of forms, searching only after its categorial differentiations, it would soon be evident that it is not fundamental enough for that. Indeed it proves itself lacking in homogeneity. Man is also an animal, but not a plant. Both animals and plants share in the properties of material things. But a society of men is not *a* man. It includes man and transforms him throughout but is, itself, something completely different. And the same applies to a still higher degree to history. Therefore, another division must be made by which the categorial difference between the rungs becomes unequivocally comprehensible in exact conformity to the phenomena.

At this point we need not scruple simply to accept the Cartesian dichotomy of the world into *cogitatio* and *extensio*. This division is intended to determine a categorial difference of regions. Not only are "soul and body" here placed in contrast to each other, but a non-spatial inner world, intelligible to consciousness with its multiplicity of contents and acts, is opposed to the spatial outer world. By their whole mode of being these two realms are different and, therefore, do not gradually shade off into one another. Even their mode of being given shows the same heterogeneity. Hence Descartes, using the conceptual language of his time, could declare them "substantially" different.

Actually the difference which here fixes a clear-cut boundary line lies not in the kind of substance but in completely
different basic categorial conditions. That, however, is a matter for later consideration. On the other hand, it is important
to note that the difference between these two realms of being
does not coincide with any one step of our order of rungs.
Rather, it cuts straight through the human being; indeed, it
seems to shatter the unity of structure also in regard to the
higher animals. For it is impossible that man alone should have
psychic life, although only in him does it reach a higher stage
of development. But within the human being, truly heterogeneous strata of being are marked by the Cartesian division
line. The essential point in this, however, might be that this
duality in no way removes the unity and wholeness of the
human being.

Meanwhile this is only the first step. Both realms of being
are divided still further. The spatial outer world is divided
into two strata: on the one hand, that of inanimate things and
physical processes; on the other, that of the animate beings.
The realm of the non-spatial, however, first understood as the
inwardness of consciousness, contains in itself another differentiation of strata—one not so easily grasped and actually
grasped only late—that of the psychic and the spiritual.

The latter difference is best revealed by the community of
spiritual content such as is contained in speech, knowledge,
evaluation, legal order, and so forth. Such contents transcend
the consciousness of the individual, and in their totality are
never exhaustively contained in a single human consciousness.
But there is no collective consciousness embracing the individuals. Such spiritual content then can no longer be characterized as a psychic phenomena. It belongs to another sphere
with another mode of being. And this intersubjectivity arises
not only in connection with such things as factual exchange

of views, communication, or the framing of objective concepts. Rather, the thought such as it takes shape in the consciousness of the individual is elevated to this objectivity so that the individual is able to become conscious of that characteristic of universal validity which his thought has for every thinking being.

In the consciousness of modern man, who from youth on grows up into a common spiritual world, nearly everything is formed as to its content and elevated to objectivity. Thereby consciousness liberates itself from subservience to vitality and becomes a spiritual consciousness. It thus enters into a certain contrast with that primary consciousness which is determined by instinctive life and harnessed to its service. The latter may be called "spiritless consciousness." It is not extinguished in the fully developed human being but persists in the background of his spiritual consciousness. Occasionally it may break forth all of a sudden, perverting the objective order of the spirit. In the young child this spiritless consciousness is the dominant one, just as it is in the higher animals, and there is little doubt that through long periods of man's prehistoric development his consciousness was predominantly a spiritless one.

In this manner we obtain four main strata which embrace the whole sphere of the real world with the multiplicity of its ontic structures. Their differentiation corresponds to the realms of phenomena articulated according to the most important differences between heterogeneous spheres of objects. The sciences, in like manner, split up into interrelated groups of fields according to the same differences. From the fields of exact knowledge of inorganic nature the biological sciences are set off by a clear demarcation line. These are followed by psychology with its various branches, from which in turn the *Geisteswissenschaften* proper distinguish themselves by subject matter and methods (the sciences of history, language, literature, art, laws, and the like).

Just as the groups of sciences are variously interrelated and by necessity mutually overlap, so their fields of subject matter are interrelated, too, and their boundaries form no impassable barriers. In particular this is true of the border fields between psychic and spiritual being. But in regard to the relationship of inanimate and animate nature, too, the boundary should not be drawn dogmatically so as to cut the two fields asunder, let alone put between them an unbridgeable chasm. At most, a wider hiatus may be assumed to exist between the organic and the psychic. That seems, at least, to be justified because of the profound heterogeneity of the spatial-material in comparison to the non-spatial and nonmaterial. But it must not be forgotten that the hiatus depends only on the contrast of these categories, while in the human being psychophysical unity is present and can be observed in man's activity and experience throughout.

The drawing of a boundary is, after all, not as ontologically important as is the discovery of the special nature of the strata themselves. For every attempt to determine the principles of these strata inevitably leads to categories. Then it is found that every one of these strata has its own peculiar ontological categories which nowhere simply coincide with those of the other strata. Indeed, it is the difference between the dominant ontological categories which distinguishes the strata from each other. So metabolism, assimilation, automatic regulation, and reproduction of the individuals clearly distinguish the stratum of the organic from that of physical-energetic processes and dynamic structure. For these do not reproduce themselves, and they regulate themselves only by oscillation around a previously established center of balance. Likewise, their maintaining of themselves temporarily is due not to a

constant renewal but rather to the inertia of a substantial carrier.

It is, moreover, characteristic of these four main strata of
reality that they not only do not coincide with the levels of
actual structures (inanimate object, organism, man, and so
forth) but rather cut across them. They are not only strata of
the real world as a totality but also strata of the actual structures themselves. Man, for example, is not only a spirit; he
has a spiritless psychic life, too. He is also an organism and is
even a material structure of the same nature as other inanimate
things. He reacts to certain stimuli instinctively like an animal,
and, like an animal, too, he propagates his species, just as he
experiences thrust and counterthrust like a material object.
The organism, for its part, possesses, besides the quality of
being animate, also the general character of physical materiality. Indeed, only thus is it possible that the organism's life
process should consist essentially in a change of materials.
Nonetheless, looked at ontologically, the organism consists
of only two strata, while man embraces all four strata. In the
higher orders of the animal kingdom the threefold division
already begins to manifest itself inasmuch as the emergence
of consciousness adds another level to organic life.

Not man alone embraces all four strata of being. It is the
same with society and the historical process. The unity of a
people is rooted in the organic unity of the race. Also peoples
of mixed race are not entirely lacking this unity. It always
rests upon the preservation of an inheritable type through the
succession of generations, the equilibrium of dispositions being guaranteed by continual crossing. The life of the race is
in turn supported by the entirety of physical conditions
through which alone it can persist. On top of this the consciousness of the individual first rears itself. This, again, is the
bearer of a common spiritual life in which all productivity, all

development of society, and all historical activity have their foundation. This piling up of the layers of being does not rend the human community asunder nor does it make it inhomogeneous. Its unity is rather a complex and stratified whole. Indeed it is comprehensible only through the interrelatedness of the strata.

The same holds true for the process of history. There has been much debate about it, especially about what form of determination is dominant in history. In this matter the theories have nearly always been extreme ones. They tried either to explain the course of human history causally or to derive it from directive ideas which human beings themselves posited and actively brought to realization. Facts can be adduced in support of both views, and yet both remain one-sided. Philosophers have surrendered either to historical naturalism or a historical teleologism. The truth is that both forms of determination overlap and variously co-operate in the process of history. But even this does not suffice, because in many cases organic determination also enters into play and assumes a great importance. All instances of power running its course, all expansion, all wealth of talent, yes, even every manifestation of decadence is determined by it. One must therefore get accustomed to the idea that these powers which determine the course of history belong to different strata. Everything here depends upon a right understanding of their interlocking.

The tiers of reality form a stratified order not only within the unity of the world but also in the actual structures of the higher layers, in such a fashion that the lower strata are always included in the higher ones. And this relation obviously cannot be reversed. The organism cannot exist without atoms and molecules, but these can exist without the organism. So the human being contains within himself all strata of being, and it is an empty abstraction to regard him only as a spiritual being. In the highest actual structures of the real world the whole hierarchy of the world recurs on a smaller scale. Hence they look like minute worlds and, accordingly, are understood as microcosms by certain philosophical theories. This analogy, however, must be accepted with caution. It has even misled some into a perverted understanding of the world in analogy to man. This leads to anthropomorphism. The task should rather consist in first reducing the analogy to its proper measure. For this, considerations of a totally different nature are needed.

In the meantime much is won by clearly distinguishing between the character of the strata of being on the one hand and the structures of the hierarchy on the other. Without that distinction it is impossible to understand the differentiation of the categorical edifice. Otherwise it would always remain incomprehensible why inanimate object, plant, animal, and man all have a structure in part identical and in part completely different—different not by mere gradation but in the sense of basic heterogeneity and incomparability. It is rank folly to oversimplify this amazing fact in order forcibly to subject the vast variety of the forms of reality of which the world consists to the rational postulate of unity. Phenomena must not be tampered with. In order to stand up, a theory must be in harmony with them, or else it is wrong.

It must be understood that the deepest heterogeneity does not preclude the unity of essential interrelatedness, both in regard to the single strata of the actual structures as well as in regard to the whole of the world. Yes, even the converse might conceivably be the case: The forms of unity might rise to a higher level along with the increase of multiplicity and heterogeneity. Indeed, it might be that the higher structures (such as man and society) are precisely the forms of a higher unity. The "height" of the unity would then consist in the integration into the wholeness of a total structure (that is, of a structure of higher order) a multiplicity both greater by itself and including the greater number of levels.

That, however, is not possible if the hierarchy of ontological structures exists without a common basis. On the other hand, it is entirely possible if there are strata of being which cut across the strata of actual structures and if, accordingly, the more strata the actual structures possess, the higher they are. The lowest tier, in that case, would consist of one stratum only, the next highest of two, and the highest would contain all strata. All actual structures, no matter on what level, would then be stratified "from the bottom up." And they would be homogeneous in that they all contain the same basic stratum, while the highest levels would share with all the lower levels these other strata which constitute their inner structures.

Herewith the main weight in the hierarchical order of the world is shifted from the levels of actual structures to the strata. It is necessary to subject these strata to a closer examination. Two tasks then arise as the most important ones. First, the basic determinants of the single strata, that is, their categories, must be worked out. Second, their mutual relations are to be determined. The first task is that of categorial analysis in the narrower sense; the second, that of an analysis of the strata. The former is predominantly concerned with the categorial difference of the strata; the latter, predominantly with their interrelatedness. For inasmuch as the strata are superimposed one upon the other in all the higher structures, the mode of their superimposition must be pointed out. At the same time the border lines between the strata must be drawn out. For these are by no means of the same kind everywhere.

These two tasks can be separated perhaps in the program of the work but in no way in its execution. One must rather attack them together. For actually the interrelations as well as the border lines between the strata are dependent on the categories which are dominant in them. And since the single categories are by no means easily discovered, their interrelations, which cross the boundaries between the strata, furnish an important clue for the discovery of categories. In view of this we must look for categories which are common to all strata. Such categories are significant as providing the universal foundations of being; at the same time they form the connecting links in the hierarchy of the world. Hence they may rightly be called "fundamental categories."

While ontology occupies itself with these tasks, it must at the same time guard against false steps. Since ancient times, philosophy has been on the track of ontological categories, even though it designates them by ever different names. Nor is the stratification of the world a new idea. Actually, many categories were discovered early, and later research, based on a richer experience, has borne out these discoveries. If we are asked why a great many ideas which were considered certain before were found to be wrong later, so that they are useful now only as instructive mistakes, no summary answer pointing out one single reason can be given. The reasons are many, because the sources of errors are many. And these it is necessary to detect. For it is clear that otherwise we might fall again into the same mistakes.

Preparatory work of this type is the task of a critique. Therewith a further basic trait of the new ontology comes to light. In contrast to the old dogmatic ontology, it must claim to be a critical ontology. And if perhaps the new ontology can only partly justify this claim, it must at least pave the way toward this goal and advance in the direction of it, in order to better its claim as its work progresses.

Inevitably we shall remember here the pioneering work accomplished by Kant's critique, which was intended to clear the ground for a "future metaphysics." Kant's critical work, however, was purely an epistemological one, and the boundaries which it drew were of a general nature. It affirmed that objectively valid knowledge was limited to phenomena. Ontology, however, is not served by this. Not that ontology might not rest content with that which Kant called phenomena. For Kant meant by phenomena nothing less than empirical reality, and according to him only that which was beyond all experience should also be inaccessible to cognition. Now the new ontology is not speculative metaphysics either, and the Kantian limitation of knowability holds good for it as well as for every serious science. But ontology cannot rest content with this limitation, and, on the whole, the merely epistemological critique is not enough for it. It requires still another critique.

This other critique must start from the object. Its concern is the gaining and securing of a definition of categories which really fits the stratified system of the world. But that is not readily accomplished. For this critique bears upon the content. It must, therefore, define boundary lines separately for each category. That, of course, can only be done in the analysis of the content of the categories, and thereby what first appears as mere preparation is now drawn into the principal investigation.

However, some guiding principles of this critique can be indicated in advance. And it is they that matter first, because through them the character of the new way becomes visible, its difficulties as well as its possibilities.

Chapter VI

Old Mistakes and New Critique

INSTEAD of tracing the manifold erroneous conceptions and applications of categories, we shall confine ourselves to one very old and ever recurrent prejudice in order to show what errors of this sort are like.

Ancient atomism was the first to develop a theory about the material structure of bodies, their peculiarities and changes. It accomplished this by laying down two principles which complemented each other, the principles of the "atoms" and the "void." These principles proved productive, recurred in numerous later theories, and, with some modifications, have survived even in modern physics. But the old atomism did not stop there. It applied its findings to other types of objects, to organic life and to the Soul. Thereby it erred and became materialism.

The thesis that the soul consisted of atoms and moved in the same space with bodies was bound to remain a mere assertion. None of the manifestations of psychic life, not even the simplest feelings, emotions, or ideas, could be explained by this hypothesis. The boundary of the field within which the two principles had been found was crossed, and outside this boundary they showed themselves powerless. Through them, phenomena of a nonmaterial nature could not be grasped. The amazing thing, however, is that despite this failure, materialism survived as a theory. In the eighteenth century, during the period of Enlightenment, it still played an important role. Even in the nineteenth century it experienced a revival in Ludwig Büchner's doctrine of *Matter and Energy* and related theories.

The same violation of boundaries, only in the opposite direction, is found in the Aristotelian philosophy and in all the theories which have followed it until today. The purposiveness which characterizes human action is stretched so as to cover all processes of the world, including the physical processes. The result is a universal teleologism. Just as in materialism a category of the lowest ontological stratum is transferred to the higher strata, so here a category of the highest stratum is transferred to the lower ones. In this case the effect of the transfer is of an opposite nature. Once a teleological principle of natural processes is accepted it is very easy to "explain" by its means a multitude of unintelligible relationships. The trouble with this explanation is that it remains arbitrary and cannot withstand criticism. Purposiveness presupposes an intelligence positing purposes and operating in accordance with them. Such an intelligence would have to be assumed either as being immanent in things or as ruling over them. In point of fact, this method has always led to theistic, or at least pantheistic, conceptions.

This transgression of boundaries "downwards"—as we may call it in contradistinction to the materialistic transgression "upwards"—is in no way connected with the category of purpose alone. It is connected with all the categories of the spirit (intelligence, reason, will, evaluation, and others). There is a long series of metaphysical systems which make the spirit the foundation of the whole world and then try to explain everything with such categories. Herein Schelling and Hegel are closely akin to the old masters of Scholasticism, no matter how much they disagree in other matters. And here the same effect is noticeable. It is easy in this way to frame a unified picture of the world, but in no way is it a picture of the real world. Sooner or later this becomes evident by a collision with the phenomena. Since phenomena cannot be argued away, such world pictures must simply collapse.

The mistake under discussion is of a still wider scope. There is an arbitrary transfer of categories to other strata not only from the lowest and highest strata but also from the middle strata. So a biologism arises which interprets everything organologically (for example, the human community and even cosmic systems). Further, there is a psychologism which desires to explain the whole spiritual world by psychic conditions and processes. The transfer from the psychic can also be directed downwards. This is what happened in Leibniz's metaphysics. The principle of the monad was derived from the phenomenon of psychic unity and then ascribed in various degrees to the lower strata.

Noteworthy in all these examples is the fact that everywhere an adequately conceived principle is laid down—a principle adequate for those fields of objects within which it was discovered and for which it was originally calculated. The mistake in all these cases lies only in the generalization. Using a more epistemological expression, we may assert that the mistake lies in a false application to fields with which the discovered principle has nothing to do and in which it has never been discovered. And always the boundaries violated by this false application are the ontic boundaries between strata.

There is probably nothing more human than this kind of

error. The most fertile minds in history have succumbed to it, and quite understandably so. For it is they who are the great discoverers. The delight of discovery seems to ravish the discoverer beyond the realm of his discovery. What he has found in one ontological stratum will seem to him to apply to all the other strata. Also there enters into play the natural tendency of viewing the world in as unified a picture as possible and, if at all feasible, of deriving all strata from the same principles. This tendency may be called that of monism. It involves a prejudice in favor of simplicity.

But the world of reality is not so fashioned. This interpretation fails to do justice to its diversity. If categories of one stratum are applied without careful examination to lower or higher strata, the world is simplified in thought, and thereby the whole world picture is falsified. This error is especially understandable where the adjacent stratum is still categorially unexplored and invites assimilation because of the similarity of certain phenomena. But the transfer still remains a dangerous intellectual adventure and can easily do violence to a whole ontological stratum. This is what happened in the case of the determination of the organic—we have shown above why it forms such an insoluble riddle. Theories here are quickly at hand to fill the lacuna of our knowledge by borrowing principles either "from above" or "from below" and applying them without hesitation. The mechanistic interpretation transferred to the organism the principle of causality; the vitalistic interpretation did the same with the teleological principle, both hoping thus to solve the problem.

This is not to say that every category is limited to one single stratum. The last-mentioned example makes that quite clear. For undoubtedly also in the organic process the simple relation of cause and effect holds good. So the application of the principle of causality is here in order, although this principle stems from a lower ontological stratum (that of the inorganic). This transfer becomes faulty only when it claims exhaustively to explain by the principle of causality that unique type of determination of an evolutionary process which derives from a system of dispositions. This is not possible, because the "prospective" character of a system of dispositions demands a different form of determination from the causal one.

It is necessary to proceed cautiously. In general the sphere of applicability cannot be limited for all categories to that stratum in whose territory they were discovered and where they stand most clearly revealed in actual structures. There is also a genuine ontic overlapping of strata. This overlapping is not arbitrary; it is determined by very definite relations between the strata. In the last analysis, the case is a different one with every category or group of categories. It is impossible to tell at first sight whether a category discovered in a certain field is limited to this field or whether it reaches into the neighboring strata. In every particular case this requires a special examination. The adjacent ontological strata must be analyzed to see whether or not they contain the same category. Thus only can that deeply engrained error, the violation of boundaries and the artificial simplification of the world picture, be successfully combated.

Clearly a new critique becomes a desideratum here. This critique, too, will aim at delimiting objective validity, just as the Kantian did. For it, too, the validity which must be limited is the validity of previously discovered categories. The difference consists only in that the border line cannot be drawn for all categories summarily, but must be determined for each one separately; also the criteria of validity are furnished by ontological instances rather than by cognitive ones. The particular character of the ontological strata and their mutual intercategorial relations determine the scope of a category. To that extent, and also from the point of view of method, this desideratum of a new critique is an ontological rather than an epistemological requirement.

For the stratified structure of the world, such a critique must provide an objective measuring rod to determine the ratio obtaining in this structure between oneness and multiplicity. All metaphysical systems have understood this ratio in far too simple a manner. As the heterogeneity of the strata seemed to them an opaque and irrational fact, they unconditionally surrendered to the rational desire for unity and uncritically generalized what they had caught sight of in one particular field. This holds true for the transfer from the stratum of the spirit to the lower strata as well as for the transfer from the stratum of matter to higher strata. It also holds true for all the intermediate types of transfer exemplified in one-sided world pictures. It could almost be said that it holds for all metaphysics that ever existed. In fact, the speculative systems, practically without exception, belong under two types: metaphysics "from above" and metaphysics "from below." Through this sort of generalizing the world was made readily comprehensible and at the same time was cut to the measure of human reason. The law once found could be laid down as universally valid, and deductions could be made from it. Thus metaphysics became a deductive system.

It is these highly deductive systems which have robbed philosophy of the firm foundation of a scientific method. They all lasted only a short time and had to yield to the very first attack of criticism. Their foundation proved untenable: The generalized categories were taxed far beyond the limits of their usefulness. The new ontology tends to eliminate every deductivity of this type. That, of course, can only be achieved if the presupposition of this deductivity, the use of generalized categories as points of departure, is likewise eliminated. Thus the fact that the method of the new ontology is analytic assumes in this connection a new significance: The categories themselves must first be attained by induction. So the new way does not lead from them downwards but in every case first upwards to them. And there always remains in that which is reached by this sort of procedure an element of the hypothetical which in turn needs to be verified by other data.

The monistic rational desire to comprehend the whole world as in itself unified and homogeneous can, of course, not be satisfied in this manner. But is the real world as homogeneous as rational desire would like to see it? Is it, in fact, so reasonable that human reason in its tendency to comprehend it can trust its own propensities? As long as it could be believed that a Reason comparable to human reason but elevated to the Absolute had created the world, this trust, even though daring, was meaningful. With the disappearance of this belief it becomes utterly senseless. Reason's desire for unity then proves an illusion.

Yet it would be just as unreasonable and as arbitrary to go to the other extreme and deny any unity to the world. There is nothing to support this view either. It goes without saying that the world such as it is has its unified character. But it does not lie as clearly exposed to view as does the multiplicity which it embraces. And, of course, it is different in type from the one which reason tends to construct. It cannot be understood in analogy to particular objects. Least of all can it be grasped by ignoring multiplicity. For whatever its nature it surely must consist in the unity of just this multiplicity. Hence the generalizing of single groups of categories is the worst possible method of grasping it. In every quest after the unity of the world the categorial heterogeneity of the strata must be conserved under any conditions.

It is important here to make clear that unity can consist of something completely different from mere uniformity in the ontological foundations of being. It need not be a unity of principle or a unity of origin (perhaps in the manner in which Plotinus conceived it) or even a unity of just a few principles. It might rather consist in the unity of structure or in that of an all-pervasive order. Unity of the latter sort can be reconciled with far-reaching heterogeneity. But naturally it cannot be constructed a priori, nor can it be anticipated before the actual work of categorial analysis is done. It can only be the result of this work.

For this kind of ontology the prospects are not too bad. It may be said that the development of ontological categories from the first step on leads us inadvertently and unwillingly to such a unified picture of the world as though this were its natural blueprint. The mere insight that the world is a kingdom of strata in whose higher forms all the lower ones are rediscovered, unmistakably points to a lawful order of the whole.

There is also a way of defining more closely the special type of this order. The relationship of the strata to one another and, above all, the form of their overlapping must be discovered. For little is said with the simple statement of superimposition. What matters is rather whether and to what degree the strata are dependent upon one another and what the type of this dependence is. If we succeed in pointing out interrelatedness here, then clearly something of the unified character of the world of reality is also grasped.

The relationship of the strata cannot be determined except through the relationship of their categories. Even if the philosopher does not reflect on the categories as such, he makes use of them in merely comparing two neighboring ontological strata. For the comparison will trace the characteristic basic traits of each of the two strata. But in order to determine the mode of superimposition itself, or even the limits of the independence of the two strata, it is not sufficient just to examine their fundamental traits in general. It rather becomes necessary to grasp the distinctive marks of these fundamental traits as such. That, however, means that a categorial analysis of the two ontological strata is undertaken.

So all the threads of the new ontology lead to the doctrine of categories. The objectives of the more inclusive critique and the new definition of the limits of knowability in the field of ontology, the relation of homogeneity to heterogeneity in the multiplicity of being, the particular character of the ontological strata, their border lines and interdependencies, the structure and unity of the world of reality—all these depend on the ontological categories and on their intercategorial relationships. To work these out and, wherever possible, to understand them as a unified whole is not just part of the business of ontology but is its total task.

Chapter VII

Modification of the Fundamental Categories

THE analysis of the categories themselves cannot be presented within the confines of a brief summary. It must be worked out in detail, and then it will constitute a science all by itself. It may also be added that today this science is still in its initial stage. Especially in regard to the higher strata, it can as yet hardly record results worth mentioning. An exception to this is certain principal insights which, important though they are, have only a programmatic character.

It is true that at all times systematic philosophy has labored to develop categories. For in all its forms it was animated by the tendency to advance to universal principles of as fundamental an import as possible. Its findings, on the whole, consist in authentic categories. So in a sense the history of philosophy is a vast sum of attempts to reduce the world to categories. But these attempts were not made for the sake of the categories themselves, and this is why their definitions generally lacked precision. All the same, both the wealth of philosophical experience and the ever-renewed criticism provide a certain fund of accumulated work from which much can be taken, at least for a first orientation. By borrowing from the historic treasure we may single out an assortment of examples sufficiently familiar to contemporary thought to furnish the point of departure for a discussion of principles.

The view, used here as a point of departure, that the particular ontological strata have their special categorial systems whose elements cannot be transferred to other strata without closer examination, is anticipated, in part at least, in the history of thought. But we also find forecast in it a series of fundamental categories which are common to all strata. Universally known, for example, are the categories of the corporeal world, space and time, process and condition, substantiality and causality. Less well known is the mutual influence upon each other of simultaneous processes (called "reciprocity" by Kant), likewise dynamic structure and dynamic equilibrium. From these are clearly distinguished the categories of animate nature: organic structure, adaptation and purposiveness, metabolism, self-regulation, self-restoration, the life of the species, the constancy of the species and variation. These two categorial groups do not gradually shade off into each other. They distinctly form two different categorial strata corresponding to the two ontological strata to which they belong. In psychic reality the following categories play a similar role: act and content, consciousness and unconsciousness, pleasure and displeasure; then, in the realm of the spirit: thought, knowledge, will, freedom, evaluation, personality. Among the latter are equally included the basic conditions of the historical superindividual spiritual life, which, however, are more evasive and elude expression by traditional concepts.

These are examples. Of course they are not sufficient to give an idea of the strata. But from them, two things can be seen: (1) the unequivocal co-ordination of categorial strata and ontological strata; (2) the inner homogeneity and interrelatedness of the categories of each single stratum. Obviously this does not mean that single categories determine special types of actual cases while other categories determine other types. Rather, all categories of one stratum jointly determine everything and share in all particulars. In actual spiritual life, for example, thought, knowledge, will, and evaluation are not present separately but only collectively, although in various degrees according to the nature of the particular act. The association within a stratum forms an insoluble unity. As a result it is impossible to grasp a single category by itself. In isolation it can be grasped only in a one-sided and distorted manner. Many philosophical attempts starting from such an isolation have experienced this. Success depends wholly on the breadth of the base of departure within the whole ontological stratum.

As to the first point, the co-ordination of ontological strata and categorial strata, we have not yet done with it. There is not only an encroaching of some categories upon other strata as suggested above. In the serial order of strata of categories there is "at the bottom" an annex with no corresponding ontological stratum assignable to it. This annex is formed by the fundamental categories. And this their unique position in no way involves a contradiction. They, too, as a matter of course, have an ontological field on which they bear. Only it does not consist of a single ontological stratum but of the whole succession of strata. They are the categories common to all strata.

In more than one respect these fundamental categories are especially important. In the first place, on them depends the interrelatedness of the ontological strata—an interrelatedness achieved not by mere continuity or adjacency but rather "from within," through the similarity of certain permeating basic traits. In them the element of homogeneity shining through the multiplicity of strata is revealed. And herewith something of the unity of the world becomes comprehensible. Moreover, the manner in which, and the conditions under which, the categories of one stratum encroach upon other strata is more easily shown in reference to these fundamental categories. For they pervade all strata. Thus the question of a critique also depends on their getting clearly defined.

Regarding the content, however, they offer only a minimum of comprehensible determinacy. That is the consequence of their high generality. They are concretely grasped only as we pursue all their variations through the strata. At first glance they impress us as a collection of commonplaces. In fact, nearly all of them are familiar to us in life. But in life we pay no attention to them. The beginning of philosophical reflection is the discovery of the enigmatic in the self-evident.

The categories are as follows: unity and multiplicity, concord and discord, contrast and dimension, discretion and continuity, substratum and relation, element and structure. Here belong also: form and material, inner and outer, determination and dependence. Also, qualitative contraries can be added, such as identity and difference, generality and individuality; likewise, the modal categories: possibility, actuality, necessity, and their negative counterparts.

Each of these categories runs through the entire sequence of strata, varying from stratum to stratum. The unity of the organism is a different one from that of the physical body, that of the life process a different one from that of energetic processes. Again different are, higher up in the ontological order, the unity of consciousness in the shift of its conditions and contents, the unity of the human person in the variety of his deeds and fortunes, the unity of a people, a state, or any such collective structure. And to this corresponds a variation and modification in the category of multiplicity. By no means does multiplicity decrease on the higher levels. On the contrary, the higher levels are much more richly differentiated, and the higher types of unity must organize a greater and more diversified multiplicity. Therefore they are on the whole less completely master of the multiple than are the lower unities.

The other pairs of contraries undergo a similar modification. Most of them are intensified in the higher strata. This is the case, for example, with opposition (not to be understood as contradiction, which exists only in thought, but rather as actual incompatibility) and its counterpart, the forms of concord (harmony, compensation). On the plane of physical processes, there is opposition only between counteracting forces, and in every relatively stable structure (for example, in the atom, the solar system, and so forth) these counter-forces are so related to each other as to establish a balance. The simple laws of their functioning suffice for this. In the organism such laws do not suffice to maintain the balance. Here various types of processes are pitted against one another (assimilation and dissimilation), and to achieve balance a regulative power working from within is needed. This balance cannot be stabilized *in infinitum* but is limited by the individual's aging and death. One level higher up, the balance is again restored inasmuch as the mortality of the individual is countered by the reproduction (procreation) of new individuals so that the total life of the species continually goes on in the change of individuals. The strongest forms of opposition are found in spiritual life. We know them as the conflict of interests, the class struggle, the claim to power of the peoples, the moral conflicts of the individual. Here harmony is provided for neither by natural laws nor by spontaneous self-regulation. Here the balance is dependent upon the freedom of men who must first discover the method of achieving this balance.

In the same way all the fundamental categories can be traced through the system of strata. Only to this approach is the full scope of their significance disclosed. Only a survey of the wealth of their variations can exhaust their true meaning. To complete the total picture two more examples of such variation and modification may be added, both being equally instructive as to the relationship of the strata.

The first example concerns the well-known opposition of form and matter. Here it is not a question of an absolute, ultimate, insoluble matter in the sense of the material principle of the earliest metaphysics, nor is it a question of a realm of forms of identical elevation such as the Aristotelian one. As categories, form and matter are strictly relative to one another, in such a manner that all form can be matter for a higher form and all matter can be form for a lower matter. The series thus arrived at is a continuous superimposition of forms, with each form serving as matter for another form superimposed upon it. Nature is clearly constructed on this principle of superimposition. The atom is the matter of the molecules but is itself a formed structure. The molecule is the matter of the cell, which in turn is the matter of the multicelled organism. But this rising series of forms does not continue unhampered. It does not run in one straight line through the whole stratified system of the world. Rather, there are incisions interrupting the sequence of superimposition. This happens, for example, on the border line of organic and psychic life. While the organism includes atoms and molecules, transfiguring them into new forms, consciousness excludes the organic forms, leaving them, as it were, behind it. The psychic life is, of course, a formed whole by itself, belonging to a higher type of form. Yet it does not superinform the organism (or its parts). Rather, with it there begins a new series of forms for which corporeal life with its material forms and processes is no longer matter. And one level higher, on the border line of the psychic and spiritual reality, the same relationship obtains. Psychic acts do not enter as material into the objective, spiritual structures. Rather, these disengage themselves from their substratum, winning a historical super-individual mode of being.

It follows that the enormous multiplicity of forms of which the world consists does not constitute a simple series of super-impositions. And this is especially instructive in regard to the element of heterogeneity in the unity of the world. Expressed in terms of categorial analysis: At the just-mentioned points of incision, novel substrata, replacing lower forms, begin to serve as matter. The category of substratum—signifying not something merely relative but an absolutely irreducible ulti-mum—in a certain sense supplants the category of matter.

The categorial couple, determination and dependence, forms the other example of a characteristic variation. The two, though forming a single relationship, yet reveal two different aspects of it. This is borne out by the fact that we know much more about dependence and are aware of more different forms of it than of determination. The latter is the active, decisive moment, the hidden core of the relationship, while dependence is its more conspicuous and external counterpart.

Here no hasty conclusions must be drawn as to the causal relationship. Cause and effect constitute only one among many forms of determination. Rather, the general basic re-lationship can be characterized by the *principium rationis sufficientis* which affirms that nothing occurs in the world that does not have its ground in something else. This rela-tionship is also found in the realm of thought (as cognitive ground) and in the mathematical relationships (known, for instance, from the Euclidian mode of demonstration). But in neither case is it a causal relationship. The universal law of determination asserts no more than that nothing in the world exists by chance in the ontic sense. Everything depends on conditions and occurs only where these are fulfilled. If, however, all conditions are fulfilled, they form a sufficient reason, and the event is bound to occur.

The modification of determination and dependence in the strata is of an ontologically central significance. For on each level the basic relationship assumes a new form, and these special forms or types of determining relationships form everywhere the most important elements of the categorial strata. On the lowest level we have the dependence of the subsequent upon the precedent, running parallel to the stream of time where every stage of the process is both the effect of preceding causes and the cause of subsequent effects. This chain of stages forms the so-called causal sequence which as a matter of principle goes on without beginning or end and thus leads to the antinomy of "the first link."

Besides causality, and located with it on the same level, we find the reciprocal causality of the simultaneous. Its meaning consists in the cross relationship of causal chains which otherwise would run independently of one another. Thereby the single processes in the course of events join in the unity of a total process. In it the partial effect, occurring at a certain stage, is always codetermined by all other factors belonging in the same cross section.

One level higher, in the organic, a new determining form enters. It expresses itself in the purposiveness of the partial functions viewed in their mutual relations, in the self-regulation of the whole, and in the self-restoration of the individual, whose operation is guided by a system of dispositions. Here, also, the partial occurrence is determined by the whole. The internal structure of this determination we do not know, the particular nature of the *nexus organicus* being at present unknowable. Hence the attempts to understand it either as a complex causality or as purposiveness have both proved to be misleading.

Just as unknown is the inner nature of the determination of psychic acts. Here, too, attempts have been made to reduce everything to causality. But this will not suffice. It is true that causality is involved in the genesis and progress of acts. But the peculiarity of even the simplest psychic reaction cannot be exhausted by this explanation, much less the nature of the spontaneous autonomous tendencies of psychic life. Here again we know only of the presence of a special type of dependence but are unable to identify the form of the corresponding determination.

Regarding our knowledge at the level of spiritual life we are in a better position. Here we know exactly at least one form of determination, the teleological one which encompasses the whole realm of conscious behavior, including moral will and action. The teleological nexus is not simply the reversal of the causal nexus. Its structure is considerably more complicated. Three stages can be distinguished: the conception of a purpose, the choice of means, and the realization of the purpose through the means. The first two stages take place in the consciousness; the third is an actual process taking place in the outer world. The middle stage is actually the characteristic one, for the choice of means proceeds from the conceived purpose backwards to the first act with which realization commences. This retrodetermination of the means has the result that the teleological process is determined by its end (the purpose).

Several other forms of determination occur in spiritual life. One of them is the determination by value. Values determine the will, not with necessity, but only as a demand. The will need not follow this determination, nor can the will remove

it. Complementary to this there is another form of determination, the self-determination of the will, on the strength of
which it decides for or against the demand. We are accustomed to regard this self-determination as freedom of the will
and thereby denote the condition under which alone account-
ability and responsibility exist in human beings. But in life
we usually associate with it the idea of an uncertainty. Freedom seems to involve an undecided alternative. But that is by
no means enough for the ethical problem of will and action.
The free will is not the undetermined will but rather the
"determining" one. There is a positively determining moment
in it, and this precisely is the important thing. What is hidden
ontologically in the so-called freedom of the will is nothing
less than a new, unique, and obviously higher form of determination. And the great problem of the freedom of the
will, about which the strife of theories and points of view
will never cease, does not consist in the question of whether
the will has a field of indeterminacy for it to play in but rather
in the totally different question of how self-determination in
it can coexist with the lower types of determination.

Chapter VIII

The Strata Laws
of the Real World

THE examples just cited can serve here as no more than suggestions. Nevertheless they allow us to frame a fairly faithful picture of the role which fundamental categories play in the structure of the world. The first impression, according to which we seemed to be dealing here with mere commonplaces, disappears very quickly as we start to consider the immense multiplicity of variations which these categories undergo. This enables us to discover that the role played by them in the order of ontological strata is one of unification as well as of differentiation. They determine both the oneness and unity of the whole and the heterogeneity of the different levels.

In addition these categories show that the integration into unity of the ontological strata rests fundamentally on the fact that elementary categories penetrate upwards into the field of far higher structure and that this penetration involves their continual modification. Every one of these elementary categories, in recurring in one stratum after another, takes on something of the peculiarity of the stratum. And this is quite understandable. For each ontological stratum has its own categorial system whose elements are closely interrelated. The categories of one stratum do not determine the concrete particular separately, but jointly. As the elementary category enters this community of specific categories it adopts their collective character and is modified accordingly. In an ontological region where metabolism, self-regulation, self-restoration, and adaptation reign, the forms of unity, the kinds of opposition, harmony, continuity, and determination cannot be the same as in another region where process and condition, substance and mathematical determination, reign. The unique character of the stratum tinges the element which passes through it.

If this is so, a factor of independence in the particular strata must counterbalance the pervasive elements. To understand adequately the relationship of strata we must define this other factor in an equally general manner as has been done in the case of the "penetrating" elements, and we must illustrate it by examples taken from specific categories. Here again the variations of the fundamental categories offer a wealth of material. The ascending series of unities and the correspondingly expanding types of multiplicity show clearly how with every step something absolutely new, a categorial novelty, appears and exceeds the lower type. In regard to the series of types of determination, it is especially evident that the higher type is nowhere exhaustively included in the lower. The prospective functioning of the system of dispositions in organic development is not exhausted by causal relationship. The conception of a purpose and the retrospective choice of means in consciously purposive action form something completely new over and above the two other forms of determination—and so on up to the self-determination of the will. Finally, this peculiarity of the series of telescoping forms stands most clearly revealed in the fact that the forms super-inform one another, or, where superinformation gives out, that they are superimposed upon one another. The appearance of a higher type of form in relation to which the lower type is reduced to a material or even to a supporting base—this precisely is the emergence of novelty.

The relationship to each other of the specific categories shows the same picture even more clearly. Self-regulation and self-restoration constitute an unmistakable novelty compared to physical process and its mathematical-quantitive determinacy. Act and content of psychic life are also a novelty in comparison to the organic processes. Again novelties in relation to these two types are the creations of the communal spiritual life, such as language, knowledge, law, and morality, which persist independently of the psychic acts of the individual and are handed down in history by tradition.

On the basis of such an orientation the rule which determines the relationship of the strata to each other regarding their content can be summarized without difficulty under a number of main points. Since we are here concerned with the principles of the ontological strata, the laws themselves depend on the categories alone, and they are primarily laws of categorial stratification. But, as categories do not have an independent existence beside the particular, their laws bear most clearly upon the mutual relationships of the ontological strata themselves.

(1) In the superimposition of ontological strata, there are invariably present those categories of the lower stratum which recur in the higher. But never are there categories of a higher stratum which recur in the lower. The encroachment of categories of one stratum upon another is upwards only, not downwards.

(2) The recurrence of categories is always a limited one. It does not hold good for all categories of the lower stratum and does not in every case include all higher strata. At a certain level there is also a cessation of recurrence.

(3) With their encroaching upon higher strata the recurring categories are modified. They are superinformed by the character of the higher stratum. Only a basic categorial moment goes through the change without suffering alteration.

(4) The recurrence of lower categories never determines the character of the higher stratum. This character always rests on the emergence of a categorial novelty which is independent of the recurrent categories and consists in the appearance of new categories. The modification of the recurring elements is contingent upon the emergence of novelty.

(5) The ascending series of ontological forms constitutes no continuum. Since, at certain points of incision in the series, the categorial novelty affects many categories at a time, the ontological strata are clearly marked off against each other. This demarcation is the "distance of strata"—a phenomenon characteristic of their hierarchical order.

The foregoing critical discussion has shown that categories in general are not transferable from stratum to stratum. That does not exclude the existence of categories which are common to several strata. Indeed, the uniqueness of the fundamental categories consists in their covering all strata. Something similar is true of numerous specific categories, but not of all. There is no general rule about what a category must be like in order to transgress other strata. The only rule that can be laid down is formulated in the law of recurrence: Transgression is only upwards, not downwards. The penetration into other strata is unilateral and irreversible. Only the lower categories penetrate through the higher strata, not the higher into the lower.

So time, process, and causality penetrate into all the higher strata. Also organic life is a temporal process, and in it, too, causality, as determination of the subsequent condition by the precedent one, obtains. The same is true also for the realms of psychic events, and even spiritual life in its historical actualization runs its course in the same temporal medium. It is a total process in which every particular stage has its causal result. But this in no way holds true for all the categories of the physical, material world. Although mathematical laws and substantiality reach into the realm of the organic, they play only a minor role there. The organism has other laws, and where conservation takes place it does not rest on inertia (neither of matter nor of energy) but on active self-restoration. More important here, however, is the role of spatiality. Unlike temporality it does not penetrate into the psychic or spiritual spheres but "breaks off" at the border line between the organic and the psychic.

That is what the second law says: There is such a thing as the "breaking off" of recurrence at a certain level. The category of space is the characteristic example. We are accustomed to regard space and time as co-ordinate, basic moments of the real world. Ontologically this is incorrect. Ontologically considered, time is of far greater categorial power. It penetrates to the highest stratum. Also, the living spirit (actualized both in persons and in superpersonal historical structures) exists only in the form of becoming. It, too, has its birth, duration, and decline. Space, on the other hand, is common only to the two lowest strata. Consciousness, even at its lowest stage, is completely non-spatial.

This difference in the behavior of the various categories

prevents recurrence from becoming a universal law. It is confined to a limited number of categories. Yet there is no complete lack of rules. On the basis of the sequence of strata it can be shown that the breaking off of certain groups of pervasive categories takes place only at certain levels. Such a level is the border line between the organic and the psychic. Here the situation is different from the one prevailing at the frontier between inanimate nature and organism. The categories of the inorganic all penetrate into the realm of the organic, although some of them play only a very insignificant role there. The reason for this is that the organism includes as integral parts the dynamic structures of masses ordered to one another, superinforming these structures by virtue of its own more elevated structure. Alone with these inferior structures it also appropriates their categories. It can do so only within the same space and the same temporal process. Were not the organism itself spatial and material, and did it not have the temporal structure of a process like these other structures, it would be unable to integrate them into itself.

This relation of "superinformation" is, however, not typical of the "distances" between the strata. The psychic life is no superinformation of corporeal life. It does not integrate the organic processes and does not use them as integral parts. It is supported by these organic processes and influenced by them. But they continue below it. There may be a consciousness of metabolism or growth, but only in the sense in which there is a consciousness of external objects and processes. These, as objects of the consciousness, are located outside the consciousness. Neither as acts nor as content do they become part of its existence.

All this goes to show that act and content are of a categorially different kind. They possess neither spatiality nor materiality, nor even substantiality. The "inner world" which is built up out of them—the world of experience, feeling, perception, thinking—is an ontological region "above" organic structure, but it only rests "upon" it as on its ontological basis. It does not consist "of it" as of its material. In contradistinction to superinformation, this relation of one stratum put on top of another may be styled "superimposition."

A fact noticed before becomes evident here. The building up of the real world is no homogeneous sequence of superinformations. It cannot be represented by the generalized relationship of two of the fundamental categories, form and matter alone. All theories which try to do this break down at the psychophysical border line. The type of unity embodied in the world is not that simple. It becomes clear that there is no basis for the metaphysical apprehension that ontology with its law of recurrence might minimize the irreducible uniqueness of psychic and spiritual being, thus advocating a disguised materialism. Just as baseless is the opposite fear, that ontology might rest content with heterogeneous elements without concerning itself with their unity. It is precisely the concern of the new ontology to arrive, uninfluenced by any kind of prejudice, at a well-balanced and carefully defined idea of the relationship of homogeneity and heterogeneity in the multiplicity of ontological strata.

All this is taken into account by the way in which the first three laws are formulated. There is recurrence only to a limited extent and never without modification of the categorial content. The evident limits of recurrence—that is, such limits as can be immediately shown by reference to the phenomena themselves—are found where superinformation fails and is supplanted by superimposition. The border line between the organic and the psychic is no more than the most easily comprehended example hereof. Further up, there is still another border line of a similar type which also is not definable in terms of superinformation. It runs straight through the kingdom of the spirit and separates the personal spirit from the objective spirit. For the historical life of the objective spirit does not consist of psychic acts but only "rests" on them as on its ontological foundation. Speech, legal order, custom, morality, and science are more than parts of a consciousness. The individual receives them from the common spiritual sphere of which he becomes a participant, and then hands them on. He contributes his share to their total historical process, but he does not create for himself his own speech, morality, or science. Correspondingly, the spiritual world does not form the content of a superpersonal consciousness as is believed by some metaphysical theories. Consciousness exists only as the consciousness of the individual, but this is no adequate consciousness of the objective spirit. Besides their common racial origin, the individuals are tied together only by their common spiritual world. Every human being has his psychic life incontestably for himself. Nobody else can act or suffer for him. Consciousness divides; the spirit unites.

At the same time it is seen that the breaking off of the recurrence of certain categories at the boundaries of certain strata is not enough to explain the situation fully. The truly affirmative core in the nature of a higher ontological stratum obviously does not consist in the cessation of lower categories only, but in the emergence of higher categories. That is what the fourth of the laws of stratification, the law of novelty, expresses. The elements penetrating "from below" are not sufficient for the uniqueness of the stratum. They merely furnish a presupposition. The essential character of the stratum depends on its own categories, that is, on those by which it differs from the lower stratum.

Such novelty in the organic sphere is to be found in the

spontaneous metabolism—an interplay of constructive and destructive processes—the development of new forms, self-regulation, the persistence of life, in spite of the death of the individual, by means of procreation and heredity. Compared with such forms of existence, material substance and physical process are merely subordinate elements. Even the causal nexus, however essential its operation also in biological processes may be, cannot constitute the uniqueness of the morphogenetic processes. It is superinformed by the organic determination as inherent in the system of dispositions. This holds true for all forms and stages of spontaneous growth, from the simple assimilation of matter up to the purposeful reactions and processes of adaptation.

The law of recurrence and that of novelty jointly determine the typical form of categorial stratification. Taken by themselves they remain one-sided. Each of them expresses one aspect of the strata relationship. Recurrence guarantees the continuity, novelty, the diversity, of the strata. The modification of the recurring lower categories is also a function of the novelty of the higher stratum. In fact, that ontological strata are distinguishable from each other at all and that there is a hierarchical order of being with discernible distances between the strata—all this depends entirely on the emergence of new categorial groups. Without the occurrence of novelty, the structure of the real world would be one single vast continuum of forms, and all difference of ontological height would consist only in degrees of complexity. There would be no room for the fundamentally different.

The interruption of the series of superinformations at the borders of the higher strata can now be seen in a different light. Here the recurrence of lower categories loses its significance. Though not ceasing completely, it is limited to a few elementary parts. An abundance of novel traits, consisting of many categories of a higher order, takes the place of the receding lower categories. Thus it appears that the predominance of recurrence and the emergence of novelty mutually exclude each other. Obviously the more differentiated ones among the categories of the lower stratum cannot penetrate into the higher stratum in the face of such an invasion of novel categories. Of the more elementary categories, on the other hand, some will always penetrate, and the fundamental categories do so with the least difficulty.

It may be more correct to express this by a reversal of terms. A larger group of novel categories finds room only at those levels of the hierarchical order where a correspondingly large group of lower categories breaks off, and loses, as it were, its formative power. But both ways of putting the matter are metaphorical only. At present we still completely lack the elements even of a categorial dynamic on the basis of which we could decide in favor of one of the two modes of expression. Only this much can be said without risk: The occurrence of superimposition in the hierarchical order involves both a far-reaching cessation of recurrence and the powerful emergence, at an accelerated pace, of categorial novelty. The more differentiated special categories of a higher stratum obviously cannot coexist with the same type of categories of the lower stratum.

In harmony with this is the fact that aside from the fundamental categories, only a few categories of the lowest stratum (time, process, causality) penetrate unhampered through all strata of being. This accords also with the other fact that in the whole stratified order there is actually only one pure case of superinformation. It is located at the lowest border line where the organic world rears itself above the inorganic. Here the categories of the lower stratum are still little differentiated, and evidently the categorial novelty of the higher stratum is limited by them. In this manner it might possibly be explained why just at this level of being a rather plentiful supply of novel forms and laws can associate with the whole inventory of the lower forms. For even though subordinate positions are assigned to them, they all penetrate into the realm of the animate, and not one remains behind.

Chapter IX

Dependence and Autonomy in the Hierarchy of Strata

THE laws of stratification involve the rejection of old and engrained prejudices. They put an end to the strife between the extreme views on the question of whether the world is ruled by spirit or by matter. The world can be ruled neither from above nor from below, because in every stratum it includes a categorial novelty. On the other hand, it cannot consist entirely in the struggle of dualistically opposed determinations, because there is a penetration of certain basic moments, reaching up into the sphere of the spirit, and, further, because the middle strata are autonomous fields of being which refuse to submit to any generalized schema of opposition between those extremes.

However, the precise relationship of independence and dependence prevailing between the strata cannot as yet be derived directly from these laws. For this, further laws are required which, though based on the laws of stratification, are not identical with them.

If the hierarchy of strata had the character of superinformation throughout, the laws of dependence might conceivably be reduced to the laws of stratification. In that case, at each level all the lower categories would have to penetrate into the next higher stratum. This would, as has been shown, in no way exclude the occurrence of novelty. It would only restrict the variety of novel categories. That which exists in the lower level would become the matter of the higher level. Its structures would become the elements of higher structures, its laws the elementary ingredients of higher laws. In a world thus constructed, dependence and independence of the higher strata could exist jointly. But dependence—which would always be a one-sided dependence of the higher on the lower— would reign supreme.

This is not how the world in which we live is fashioned. But in certain traits the image we have sketched comes close to it. In the world there exists throughout a dependence of the higher ontological strata on the lower, but it is not based throughout on superinformation. The spirit is no superinformation of the atoms, nor is consciousness superinformation of the cells, and not all categories of the lower order are involved in this dependence. Relations of superimposition are inserted, and considerably limit the dependence of the higher strata.

But this limitation applies only to a certain type of dependence. It may be called the limitation of content or structure. There is, however, still another one—existential dependence. What this involves is revealed by certain questions which have puzzled metaphysicians since antiquity. Is there a psychic life without organic life? Is there organic life without physical-cosmic nature? Can the spirit exist without a supporting consciousness and, indirectly, without a bodily carrier and a physical world?

Though speculative metaphysics has frequently ventured upon such possibilities, they must be definitely rejected if the limitations of our experience are strictly to be observed.

Throughout we know spiritual life only as supported, bound to the consciousness of living individuals. And even though it is not circumscribed by their consciousness but, as "objective spirit," far transcends its boundaries, it still remains tied to its respective carriers, rests on them, and, when they expire, it survives, supported by other individuals. In like manner we know no consciousness without organic carriers and no organic life that is not tied to a very definite structure of inanimate nature providing air, water, and nutritive substance of various kinds. And this is not only a matter of experience. For, once the real nature of assimilation is comprehended, it becomes clear that it is necessarily tied to these physical conditions. As insight is gained into how primitive consciousness is fitted into the cycle of organic functions and how it develops in its service, it is evident that it cannot exist by itself as though in a vacuum but only as resting on a highly developed corporeal life.

This relationship of resting upon something and again being carried is obviously a universal one. It does not depend on some particular categories and, therefore, is not limited to the relationship of superimposition. There are clearly two types of dependence of the higher mode of being on the lower. The one has the function of providing matter and takes shape in superinformation. The other type consists in the relationship of supporting and being supported, embracing also superimposition. Its function is to provide a basis. In its case, the dependent is that which rests upon something else. Both types of dependence relationships evidently do not militate against the independence of higher form. The difference is only that the second function, which consists in providing a basis, is the more universal one in the structure of the world.

On the whole, the philosopher, in working out the categorial laws of dependence, must cling to the latter type. The preponderance of the lower categories is not exhausted by furnishing material for the higher categories. They do this only in part. Added to this must be the fact that the lower categories, in a different manner and quite aside from their penetrating into the higher stratum, determine the basis for its being. This stands very clearly revealed in the higher forms, in man, society, and history. These themselves are stratified structures, and in them organic life is supported by physical forces, consciousness by organism, spirit by consciousness in exactly the same way as in the totality of the world.

On the basis of this orientation the laws of dependence now become available for inspection:

(1) Categorial dependence is dependence only of the higher categories upon the lower, not conversely. Hence, the lower categories, measured by their determinative power, are the stronger ones. Strength and height in the order of strata stand in an inverse relationship.

(2) Although the categories of a lower stratum afford the basis for the being of the higher, they are indifferent in regard to them. They admit of superinformation or superimposition without requiring them. The higher ontological stratum cannot exist without the lower, but the lower can exist without the higher.

(3) The lower categories determine the higher ontological stratum either as matter or as a basis for its being. So they only limit the scope of the higher categories but do not determine their higher form or peculiarity.

(4) The novelty of the higher categorial stratum is completely free in relation to the lower stratum. Despite all its dependence, it asserts its autonomy. The superior structure of

the higher stratum has no scope "inside" the lower stratum, but "above" it.

Of these laws of dependence, the first and fourth—the law of strength and the law of freedom—stand in a mutual relationship similar to the relationship obtaining among the laws of stratification, the law of recurrence and that of novelty. For, the autonomy of the higher stratum in its relationship to the lower ones is obviously a result of the emergence of higher categories. The freedom of the latter suggests but one other point. It indicates that above the lower ontological stratum there is unlimited scope for higher and structurally superior formations of novel type. And this is by no means self-evident. It would presumably be incompatible with an unrestricted recurrence of all lower categories. But not all categories recur in the higher strata. This is due to the order of superimposition by which some of them are discarded.

The greater relative strength of the lower categories does not depend on recurrence alone, nor is it even coextensive with recurrence. The non-penetrating categories of the lower ontological strata, too, are superior in strength to the higher. They cannot be encroached upon within their field of validity by any superinformation, and all higher ontological formation is restricted in its development by the possibilities inherent in its foundation. For the whole lower ontological stratum remains a foundation even where it is not superinformed or where its structures do not provide matter for higher structures. Psychic life, too, is dependent on organism and, indirectly, on inanimate nature, although it does not take on its spatial, material forms, and the spirit is dependent on the whole ladder of lower strata. Its relationship to this its basis is one of "resting upon" and "being supported." If the body is killed, consciousness, and with it personality, is also extinguished. If a race dies out, its communal, objective-historical spirit perishes too. In the individual as well as in the human community all blossoming of the spirit exists as a supported reality. But the supporting strata do not necessarily perish when the blossom wilts.

In this sense, even without any superinformation, through the mere relationship of supporting and being supported, the ontological relationship of dependence is an entirely unilateral and irreversible one. This is exhibited most clearly in the second law of dependence, the law of the autonomy of the strata (or of "indifference").

The fact that in the vertical relationship of two strata, one superimposed on the other, the lower stratum forms the supporting basis of the higher is so obviously and directly revealed by the phenomena that it has always been recognized wherever and in whichever way the problem of ontological stratification has been attended to. But usually this is associated with the idea that the lower stratum is ordered toward the higher, being nothing but a basis for the latter. Thus the relationship "supporting-supported" is surreptitiously transfigured into a relationship of means and ends, and the lower stratum is considered as existing for the sake of the higher. In brief, the destination of supporting the higher stratum is attributed to the lower. So in man the body is regarded as something which exists for the sake of the soul, the physical conditions of life as something which exists for the sake of the body, and everything together is supposed to exist only for the sake of the spirit. In this way the dependence of the strata is actually reversed. For in the teleological relationship the means, existing only for the sake of the end, depend upon the end in the sense that they are determined by it.

All teleology of forms—represented in numerous systems from Aristotle to Hegel—makes the mistake of inverting the law of strength. It makes the higher categories the stronger ones. This corresponds to a certain dream image of the world, fondly framed by man at all times. It permits him to consider himself, in his capacity as a spiritual being, the crowning achievement of the world. In this manner he misunderstands not only the world but also his own being; and, rightly considered, this is not even to his advantage. His task is to come to terms with a world not made for him—a far greater objective and one worthy of his power of self-determination.

Such ideas are put out of court by the "law of indifference," not on anthropological, but rather on purely ontological, grounds. According to this law the lower ontological stratum is, in fact, the basis of the higher, yet its essence does not consist in its being a basis; that is to say, it is more than just a basis. It rather exists also by itself, independent of the higher stratum. It is indifferent concerning the existence or nonexistence of the higher stratum and is certainly not ordered toward it. In no way is its existence tied up with that of the higher stratum. This is the decisive point. The higher stratum, for its part, is indeed tied to the lower. Only as supported by it can it exist. This corresponds to the irreversible direction of categorial dependence invariably denoting dependence only of the higher being upon the lower one.

This indifference, then, involves the independence of all lower strata in relation to the higher. It is a total (not just a partial) independence. That is what we know from all experience, and especially from scientific experience. Inorganic nature exists in complete indifference toward the appearance of life in it. It forms an immense cosmic structure in which the conditions rendering living beings possible are extremely rare and exist only within a tiny area. And these special conditions, sporadic in the case of their cosmic status, are in no need of living beings. In like manner the animate world exists in

countless lower forms without consciousness. And consciousness, in its turn, has existed in the early period of mankind
through whole geological periods without the luxury of a
spirit.

This reflection is so simple that not many words should be
required to expound it. But strange as it may sound, it has been
so much sinned against in philosophical systems—and even today some greatly admired theories run counter to it—that it
has become necessary to formulate it with all possible care as
a categorial law. Seen in this light, the law of strength gains
its full weight, standing revealed as the "fundamental categorial law." It forms the background of the indifference, and
it is more fundamental than the law of recurrence. For it is
more general, and its scope is unlimited. Not even the law
of freedom limits it. It rather expresses the other side of the
same relationship of dependence.

The situation is not quite as simple as that in regard to the
law of matter. For not all lower being is matter of the higher.
In the case of superimposition, it is only the supporting basis,
instead of entering as content into the higher ontological form.
This is why not all lower categories recur in the higher stratum.

If, then, the degree of categorial dependence is to be determined with precision—and it is with this that the law of
matter is concerned—a dual law may be expected to correspond to the dual form of dependence. For the "resting upon"
or "being supported" of the higher strata is in no way identical
with the superinformation of the lower strata.

Against this, however, stands another consideration. For
this law is designed solely to determine precisely which elements of the higher ontological stratum are included in the
categorial dependence. Actually, even where all the lower
categories are effective in the higher stratum this dependence

extends to some few elements only, constituting, as it were, merely a thin thread of dependence. If, then, the lower stratum serves as a mere basis for the being of the higher, as in the case of the relationship of superimposition, dependence no longer involves the essence, but only the existence, of the higher stratum. The latter is determined not by the structure of the lower stratum but only by its existence. In this way consciousness and the spirit are determined by the supporting organism. They cannot exist in a vacuum but only as resting upon a basis. But structurally they are not tied to the forms and processes of the organism, because they do not include them as elements. Hence there is no need for a special categorial law of "basis" or "resting upon."

But a law of matter is needed. For through superinformation the higher structure absorbs the lower one in itself. Thereby the categorial dependence becomes one of content. And here it really is important to define more closely its extent within the higher ontological stratum. It is characteristic that here, too—in spite of the unrestricted penetration of the lower categories into the higher stratum—the higher form is only peripherally and, as it were, negatively determined from below. This is suggested by the term "matter": The dependence of higher structures in all superinformation reaches so far only as the peculiar nature of the building stones might be said to limit the possibilities of an edifice. Just as the human architect cannot, with the building materials at his disposal, construct anything he fancies or desires but only what the solidity and specific weight of his material permit, so, in the structure of the world, the higher category cannot, with the material of lower forms, build anything imaginable but only what is possible with this particular material. It cannot transform this material, according to the fundamental categorial law which says that the lower categories are the stronger ones, and by no higher power can they be canceled. This means that the lower forms of the real are, indeed, the stronger. It is they that furnish the matter in the relationship of super-information.

The implications of this situation are far-reaching. The determining power of matter does not extend beyond its limiting function, and, consequently, categorial dependence does not reach any further. What cannot be transformed can be superinformed. And the novelty which thus arises is not determined by the elements.

In this sense the law of matter might also be described as a law of the scope of the higher form. This immediately links up with the law of freedom. For the scope is only the negative condition of possible formation. This formation itself is something different.

That above some existing ontological stratum a fresh formation sets in is no matter of course. In fact the sequence of strata does not proceed *in infinitum*, but it has an upper limit just as much as it has a lower one. The reason is not lack of scope. It is incomprehensible why there should not be a free field of possible ontological formation above the spirit. We find such difficulty in imagining this only because we know no existent of a higher order and have some reason to believe that none exists. But this nonexistence must, in the last analysis, be accepted as a fact without our seeing the reason why this is so. And the same holds true for the fact that four ontological strata—no more, no less—are built one upon the other and that, accordingly, there are three strata distances which mark the beginning of a higher formation on top of a lower one.

It is not with these irreducible basic facts in the structure of the world that the fourth law of dependence is concerned. Rather it presupposes them just as they underlie the entirety of categorial laws. The laws of dependence deal only with dependence in the relation between strata, and the law of freedom concerns itself more specifically with the factor of independence that exists in this dependence.

Together with the ascending dependence itself, that is, the superior strength of the lower categories, this factor is the really significant element in these laws. The law of freedom states that in the stratified order throughout, the higher onto-logical stratum, regardless of its dependence on the lower, maintains its independence in relation to it. The reason lies in the relationship of the categories. Since the higher cate-gories are determined by the lower ones, at the most in re-spect to their matter (and throughout in respect at least to their basis for being), they must be free in relation to the lower categories by virtue of their autonomous structure. This their freedom, then, exists in spite of, and alongside of, de-pendence and does not contradict their being weaker. It has the character of genuine autonomy and, regarding its con-tent, coincides with the categorial novelty of the higher stra-tum. Its scope is clearly limited by the law of matter. It is a scope granted to the weaker in relation to the stronger and therefore lies not within, but above, the domain of the former.

Freedom in dependence—this is no contradiction. All au-thentic freedom is freedom "from" something and in opposi-tion to something. And this something must have the character of a fetter "against" which it asserts itself. Otherwise free-dom would be sheer absence of bounds and resistance, some-thing purely negative. The actual meaning of freedom, how-ever, consists in superiority over something else. And this superiority is the essence of categorial freedom. It becomes manifest in a very definite ontological priority, the priority of height.

It must be clearly recognized that without such a superi-ority no difference of height among the strata could possibly exist. And as the difference of the strata depends on their difference in height, without superiority even the strata themselves would disappear. That is what the monistic metaphysical theories have always aspired to. They level the disparity of strata by removing both novelty and the autonomy of the various strata. But thereby they ignore the heterogeneity of phenomena.

Reflecting now that the "being stronger" of the lower categories as stated by the fundamental categorial law denotes ontological pre-eminence and superiority just as much as the "being higher" of the weaker categories, we come to see that stratification involves an interdigitation of two types of ontological pre-eminence and two types of superiority. They are echeloned according to the same order but in opposite directions. The ontological superiority of strength decreases with the corresponding gain in height. So the two types of superiority move, so to speak, along separate lines, coexisting with one another in the same order of ranks without disrupting its unity. The lower categories are superior only in strength. In structure, they are the poorer. They leave it entirely undecided whether or not something is above them and even more so *what* is to be above them. They are indifferent toward everything higher. They do not produce it nor do they hinder it. But if something is above them, they support it. For it can exist only by resting upon them.

The clarification of the relationship between dependence and freedom is achieved in the second and third laws, that of indifference and that of matter. It has always been thought that dependence precludes independence. That is one of the many errors stemming from the deterministic mode of thought of an antiquated metaphysics. In ethics it has led philosophers to interpret the freedom of will as an obliteration of all dependence—a view which condemned to inevitable failure the wrestling with this problem. This view is just as misleading in regard to the problem of categorial dependence. Rather the opposite view is correct: Independence exists only in dependence. It consists in that other type of ontological superiority which can assert itself only "against" the superiority of the supporting conditions.

No matter how superior in strength the lower categories are to all higher forms, within the higher ontological stratum they can exert their influence only on that which according to its nature belongs in their realm. This, however, measured by the abundance of higher forms, is of subordinate significance. It affects only a few elementary traits which in no way constitute the peculiar nature of the higher structure. The convictions and deeds of man are not determined by the anatomic structure of the human body, although, together with the whole spiritual life of the person, they are supported by it. In the same way the design of the body is not determined by the atoms which are its components.

All such categorial dependence will in no way be curtailed. There is no objection to regarding it as absolute, which can only mean that it is an indelible dependence suffering no exception, but in no way that it is a total one. The superior strength of the lower structure is not to be understood in the sense that it determines "everything" in the higher being. Rather the opposite is true: The higher up in the order of strata the lower stratum makes itself felt, the thinner and more negligible do the threads of this indelible dependence become, and the more do they shrink to merely negative prerequisites.

Categorial dependence is not an impediment to autonomy but, rather, its indispensable counterweight. Though "absolute" by essence, it is only "partial" by content. But a partial dependence goes very well with partial independence. The higher formation does not require that it be wrested from the supporting foundation offered by the lower formation. This one in turn does not claim to determine the particular nature of the higher. It is both determining and indifferent, and it is so in the same sense in which the higher stratum is determined as well as autonomous.

Nothing in the history of metaphysics has been missed more consistently than this relationship, not because it is so complicated or difficult to grasp, but because its comprehension is obstructed by engrained prejudices. Reference has been made to them above. They consist in the postulate of unity and the transgression of boundaries. There is the desire to see the world as much unified as possible and the other desire to transfer the categories of one stratum to all strata. The laws of categorial dependence render possible a still deeper understanding of both these mistakes than their initial detection could afford.

Of the two types of speculative metaphysics, the one seeks to explain everything by reference to the highest forms of being; the other, by reference to the lowest forms. The one is typified by the teleology of forms, by pantheism and rationalist idealism; the other, by materialism and all related theories. By bringing the laws of dependence to bear upon these two basic types of metaphysics it is readily seen that the first violates the basic categorial law; the other, the law of freedom. Hegel's rationalist idealism, for example, makes the highest categories the strongest ones, for with him they dominate all the strata down to the bottom layer. This is the reversal of the basic categorial law, the removal of the independence and the indifference of all lower strata, and also of novelty and autonomy in the higher strata, these being left without any kind of categorial peculiarity to distinguish them from the lower ones. Such systems literally turn everything upside down.

Materialist metaphysics, on the other hand, ascribes to the lowest ontological forms the power of producing the highest. It ignores not only the novelty of the higher ontological strata and their freedom but also the limitations of recurrence. It also ignores the limitation of the determining power of the lower categories in furnishing a "basis" or, at most, a "matter."

On one point, however, materialism is less perverse than rationalist metaphysics. As a matter of principle it at least admits a penetration of lower categories into the higher strata and excludes the reverse. This penetration, however, is much more limited than materialism claims. And the categories which are the most important ones for this interpretation of the world, those of space, material substance, dynamic process, and others, break off very early at the psychophysical border line.

Again materialism in another respect is far more fatally wrong than are the opposing theories. To try to explain the lower through the higher categories, though wrong, makes sense. Its premises admitted, this way of explaining the world celebrates an effortless triumph. For the wealth of the higher categories easily lords it over the simpler phenomena. The lower categories, on the other hand, are too poor in content to do justice to the higher phenomena. Mechanical-dynamic principles are frustrated by the vital processes of even the simplest organisms. The attempt to reduce psychic and spiritual conditions to these principles is not only an erroneous, but a senseless, undertaking.

Chapter X

Objections and Prospects

FROM what has been said before it may be seen how much depends on an exact formulation of the laws of dependence. It is no exaggeration to say that with it the most important questions of metaphysics are brought to some sort of critical decision. This will be confirmed by the application of these laws to certain special problems.

First, however, an objection will naturally present itself which directly concerns the law of indifference and indirectly the basic categorial law as well. Is it really quite true that the lower ontological stratum experiences no categorial influence whatsoever from the higher categories? Or, is the categorial dependence of strata really irreversible? Is it not rather true that the higher ontological forms also play the role of determinants in the lower strata? An argument for this is the power of man over the surrounding nature, his technical skill, his ability to transform and exploit nature—in brief, precisely those features which constitute the uniqueness of the human being in the real world. This power, it may be argued, is a power of the spirit and is based on the unique categories of the spirit.

This objection should not be taken too lightly. It is not to be disposed of with the remark that the power of the spirit concerns only the "external" position of man. For precisely this external position of man and his manner of operation in the world are based entirely on his innermost peculiarity. What, then, really happens here? Man evidently transforms certain natural conditions within their own ontological realm. It is true that he can do so only within his proximate ambit, while cosmic distances are beyond his reach. Yet he has changed the face of the earth. The spirit, as a knowing, planning, and executing power, unmistakably interferes with the working of the lower ontological strata. And this does not apply to inorganic nature alone. Man raises plants and animals and thereby modifies their specific types. He also supervises his own bodily life, takes care of it, and enhances his faculties. And the same holds true for his psychic life. As an educator he takes it in hand and molds it to suit his purposes. He works on his own nature just as he works on the surrounding world. And, in general, it can be said that he works on nature more easily than on the spirit. The greatest obstacles are in his own nature. The hardest wrestling of the spirit is with the spirit.

Does not all this argue that the highest categories are also the strongest? This impression can even be deepened by comparing the action of animals to those of man. Within narrow limits the animal, too, transforms a small sector of its environment. It only lacks the far-reaching consciousness of consequences. Spiritual consciousness alone rises to a survey, to a detached orientation in the world, to a knowledge of the possible, and to purposive planning. It appears that in regard to power over nature the categories of the spirit are the stronger ones.

Yet it is not so. Denying those facts would be foolish. The question is how the facts are to be interpreted and whether they really contradict the thesis of the superior strength of the lower categories.

The facts here reviewed, and all related facts, testify to the interference of the spirit—and partly even of non-spiritual consciousness—with the lower ontological strata. They do not testify to an interference with their categorial structure and autonomous laws. But everything depends on this difference. The laws of dependence are not at variance with the ordering of things of a lower stratum by powers of the higher. Such ordering is nothing more than that superinformation which is always possible within the limits set by matter (that is, the lower order). The laws of dependence militate only against the alteration or transformation of lower categories, that is, of the basic laws and forms of a lower ontological stratum, by the higher categories.

The human spirit can in manifold ways transform particular actual structures and particular conditions of nature, and the more elementary the structures upon which it impinges, the greater its impact. But in no way can it transform the laws themselves. Over the categories determining the lower structures it has no power.

This is of crucial importance. And as we become more intimately acquainted with the relationships of which the quoted facts are illustrative, these very facts will be found to provide the fullest, most indubitable confirmation of the laws of dependence. What does the power of the spirit consist in as far as it really rules nature? Not, surely, in opposing the power and autonomy of nature, nor in fighting it or wrestling with it. In this wrestling the spirit would soon be defeated. The obverse is shown by the facts. The rule of the spirit depends on its obedience. The secret of its power over certain forces of nature within the human environment lies in its ability to understand their autonomy and to adapt itself to them in its technical creations. What the spirit prescribes to nature are but the purposes which it pursues in utilizing the forces of nature as available means. It is the higher form, as we may also put it, with which the spirit superinforms nature. But it can do so only in respecting the autonomy of the forces of nature. It cannot compel them to function differently than they do by nature. It can only exploit their own natural functioning for its purposes. For the forces of nature are indifferent in regard to purposes. They themselves do not pursue purposes, and this is why they lend themselves to being used as means toward purposes alien to them. The lower form is indifferent toward superinformation.

Furthermore, in dominating nature, the spirit continues to be just as dependent upon the categories of nature as if it exercised no dominance at all, and its own categories continue to be the weaker categories. All its creative accomplishments in the realm of nature are limited by the laws of nature. Against them it can do nothing. With them it can accomplish marvels, and in this direction its only limits are those of its inventive power.

The principle of dual superiority is here borne out by incontrovertible evidence. The elemental powers hold frail man in scorn. What in the long run secures him domination is a superiority different from theirs. The instruments of his power are foresight and purposeful activity. Nature does not command these categories. Its processes are indifferent toward their result, and its forces are blind. They cannot resist the purposeful planning of man once he has discovered their essence and knows how to harness them in the service of his ends.

Metaphysics, in broaching the problem of the power of the spirit, usually professes extreme theses. It either sees only the blind superiority of the lower powers (including those in the mind of man) and speaks of the "impotence" of the spirit, or it considers only the intelligent superiority in the creativity of man and believes in the "omnipotence" of the spirit. Both views are wrong. They contradict the phenomena of human life as well as the categorial laws. The spirit has its own kind of power, but it is a limited one. It is a power different from everything that opposes it. It is based upon the unparalleled singularity of the categorial novelty of spirit. It presupposes the whole stratification of the lower powers which it has to deal with in life while, at the same time, it rests upon them. Its autonomy is that independence in dependence so characteristic of the whole stratified order of the world.

The objection just disposed of is not the only one which raises itself against the theory of strata. The prejudices met with here are many, and most of them are connected with the postulate of unity. They conflict not only with laws of dependence but also with the laws of stratification. This is why we must now revert to them once more.

The law of recurrence, as has been shown, is not of universal applicability. Some of the lower categories break off at the border lines of the superstructure. Thereby the unity of the real world as postulated by all metaphysics seems to disintegrate. Then reflections present themselves which seem to contradict this cessation of recurrence. If the being of the higher strata rests on that of the lower, and the lower strata have their own complete equipment of categories, must not recurrence be a total one? Is it not true that the concrete actual structures of the higher ontological stratum continue to be tied up with the lower structures? They cannot wrench themselves from this basis because they are unable to exist "in the air." So consciousness cannot dissociate itself from the organism, nor the organism from the physical-material conditions, and the life of the spirit is bound up with the whole order of ontological rungs. And is not just this the meaning of the laws of strength? Do not the laws of dependence actually preclude a cessation of recurrence?

This objection cannot be effectively countered with a reference to the relationships of superimposition. For the contention is that superimposition does not limit recurrence. The inner world of consciousness, it is true, does not contain within itself the spatial processes of the organism. But the psychic events proceed in the same time as those processes and presuppose them. Psychology here tries to solve the problem by assuming a parallelism of processes. But this theory circumvents the actual problem instead of attacking it. For the psychosomatic unity of the human being is as an immediate datum, open both to the inner experience of one's own conditions and to scientific observation. Why, then, do we draw a dividing line that cuts through the human being? Strictly speaking, even the old concept of a psychophysical causality (often mistakenly referred to as reciprocal causality) is not to be dismissed. Causality exists in organic life just as well as in psychic life. But unlike the causality of masses and their motion in cosmic space it is no mechanic causality. It is not of the essence of causality to be tied to matter in space. Nor does it belong to those categories which break off at the psychophysical border line. Its reign extends upwards to the world of the spirit, the community and its history, and this does not hinder the emergence of higher forms of determination. "How" a cause produces its effect—therein lies something unintelligible even on the lowest rung. So, the impossibility of elucidating the question of how physiological processes act upon psychic processes and vice versa is no reason to deny the existence of this sort of causality.

It would thus seem to be a possibility that the border line as drawn here and defended with an array of erudite arguments is a border line only for our way of looking at things. The ontic frontier between the two strata of being would thus be obliterated. The only ontologically adequate approach would be that of the practicing psychiatrist, who as a matter of principle co-ordinates physical and psychic symptoms. And what holds true for this particular frontier must apply a fortiori to other things. In fact it has often been maintained that the transition from dynamic structure to organic structure is a continuous one. The distinction between the domain of the spirit and of psychic life has finally been made only at a late date, and even today it has not yet been clearly established.

On the basis of such considerations we might indeed speak of the total recurrence of the lower categories. Then the whole multiplicity of all lower categories would have to be included within the total categorial equipment of the higher ontological stratum. Generally it would have to hold true for every category that, once it had emerged at a certain level, from there on upwards it would never disappear again. It might then be overshadowed by the novelty of the higher stratum and, as it were, be hidden by it. But in regard to its existence it would continue even in this apparent disappearance and, at some time or other, would reassert itself emphatically. In this manner the recurrence of categories would present itself as a bundle of penetrating lines enormously increasing in density higher up. For at each level fresh categories enter. And this compactness need not involve overdetermination. Rather, it would correspond to the categorial wealth of the highest strata.

So far the picture can be developed without colliding with the phenomena. It has the advantages of a simplified picture, but also its drawbacks. It hits off very well something in the world of reality. But this something is not the hierarchy of strata such as matter, life, soul, and spirit, but rather the hierarchy of actual structures—represented by inanimate object, plant, animal, man, community—an order not identical with the order of strata but cutting across it. Psychic life does not contain within itself the organic processes, but man does. For man is a stratified being. He shares organic life with animal and plant, and material corporeality even with inanimate nature. It can be said of him that space and substance are among his categories. But these are not categories of his feelings or his volition, nor of his ethos, his speech, his existence as member of a legal order. Thus they recur in him not as a psychic and spiritual being but only as a corporeal and organic being. This, however, apparently means that their recurrence, also within the human being, breaks off at the level of psychic life.

So the border lines as drawn before reassert themselves automatically. They are not frontiers merely for our way of looking at things, but ontological borders. They do not distinguish modes of perception, but categorial structures, regardless of whether or not there is a gradual transition from one to another. It is true that there are valid methods by which human beings—and likewise the animal, the community, and history—are interpreted as unified structures. For these structures are actual units of a very definite sort. Yet they are not categorially homogeneous, but stratified, and their unity is the unity of strata. This cannot be ignored even by a reasonably monistic outlook. Zoology, anthropology, sociology, and philosophy of history, in dealing with their comprehensive structures, refer extensively to the differences of strata, using these distinctions as a matter of course because they are indispensable to them. But ontology has to deal with them as such. For the ontological strata together with their categorial systems constitute the levels of being for the whole of reality, permeating and binding together all higher structures.

The thesis of the total recurrence of categories is in harmony with the phenomena only if the higher strata together with their ontological substructures (without which, in fact, they never occur) are thought of as forming units. Then the whole order of strata will be contained within them. But uncritically to ascribe the categorial forms of the substructure to the higher strata is to distort the facts. The psychophysical unity of the human being and the all-pervasiveness of the causal nexus cannot be adduced as an argument in favor of this distortion. The basic question is rather how within the comprehensive actual structures the strata are differentiated and how they are linked together. But this question can only be answered after the categorial peculiarity of the various strata has been studied and hasty confusions have been warded off. The unity of the world is not the unity of pervasive sameness but the unity of a structure which allows for categorial heterogeneity.

This insight springs from the ontological analysis of strata. For all actually stratified structures presuppose the order of strata. In this order, however, the recurrence of categories is a limited one.

A third objection is directed against the law of strata distance. It seems that the distance placed between the ontological strata breaks up too much the continuity of phenomena. There is a close continuity of structural tiers within each stratum, and it is difficult to see why the ascending series should be interrupted at the strata boundaries. Our inability to point out transitional structures is of little account. Also, in our knowledge of the chain of structures within the vegetable and animal kingdoms numerous connecting links are missing. But these gaps do not invalidate the idea of a genetic sequence which here inevitably obtrudes itself.

This objection would be justified if the strata distances involved a disruption of the sequence of forms. But something quite different is meant: the sudden emergence of new categorial groups at certain levels. Distance is not to be understood as a gap, but qualitatively as the otherness of structure from a certain level upwards. And this idea, confirmed as it is by the phenomena, must not be surrendered. Where organic life starts, its categories emerge collectively: metabolism, assimilation, self-regulation, self-reproduction, and so forth. It is readily seen that even the most elementary living species cannot maintain itself if one of these basic functions is lacking. Hence they emerge all at once, and it is this fact of their joint appearance that constitutes the qualitative distance of the higher stratum from the lower one.

Special categorial laws are at the basis of this relationship—laws which, added to the laws of stratification and dependence, form a third fundamental factor of the whole ontological order. They may be described as laws of coherence, for they are concerned with the relationship of the categories of one stratum. What they enunciate can be stated in two sentences: (1) The categories of an ontological stratum form a self-contained whole. They determine the forms of their stratum jointly rather than singly. (2) They imply each other in regard to their content so that the emergence of one necessarily involves the emergence of the others.

This coherence, however, does not extend beyond the limits of the stratum. And if part of the categories penetrate into the higher stratum, they become integrated into the coherence of that higher stratum. This corresponds to the modification they suffer in their new association, and that is why the ontological strata are clearly set off against each other. But this is a setting off only in respect to the categorial structure.

This, finally, explains why the law of strata distance goes very well with the idea of an unbroken continuum of forms.

And should the unity of the world have the form of such a continuum, the laws of stratification and dependence would in no way contradict it. Whether it is actually so cannot be decided at the present stage of categorial analysis.

Without committing ourselves to a dogma we may take one further step toward satisfying the speculative desire for unity. The idea of formal continuity is closely associated with that of genetic sequence. But it must be noted that this idea makes a claim which at the present time philosophy can live up to even less than to the demand made upon it by the idea of the continuum, and it is a bold venture for any theory to tackle the problem of genesis. Under no circumstances will it get beyond assumptions and unverifiable hypotheses. But a problem is not illegitimate for being insoluble. In the case of the coming into being of the world, the chronologically posterior emergence of the higher ontological strata is even an inevitable consequence of the strata dependence, which is clearly a dependence of the higher on the lower. Moreover, scientifically well-established interlocking facts suggest certain perspectives which undeniably speak in favor of that idea. Life on earth, cosmologically considered, is undoubtedly a late product. It can have arisen only after the temperature had been reduced to a certain point and relatively stable atmospheric conditions had been formed. In like manner consciousness could start only in highly developed and relatively late representatives of the animal kingdom, and the spirit, even measured by the life of man, is probably still young.

So the attempt to trace vestiges of a genesis in the hierarchy and dependence of the ontological strata is quite meaningful. However, ontology, on pain of relapsing into speculative construction, must not assume the task of mapping out the evolutionary process. On the other hand, its assertions concerning the structure of the world of reality may be expected at least to admit a genetic interpretation. In view of the available evidence it should not obstruct this type of research.

Another possibility: Do the categorial laws of stratification and dependence, completely neutral as they are in regard to all genetic questions, admit of a genetic interpretation?

This question can be answered affirmatively without any hesitation. The main difficulty here would lie in the strata distances if they are regarded as fissures or gaps in the continuum of forms. This view, however, has already proved itself to be false. Neither the breaking off of lower categories nor the emergence of the novelty of higher strata disrupt the continuity of the chain of forms. So there is no reason why the latter should not chronologically also make up a uniform series. Only a simplified schema of genesis as implied, for example, in the ideas of "production" or "evolution" must be guarded against. It is quite unintelligible how a lower ontological form should "produce" the higher without containing its categories. That would lead to an interpretation of the world from "below" and would come close to materialism. Again, if the higher form is supposed to "evolve" out of the lower one, it would have to be "involved" in it to begin with. This, applied to the whole order of strata, would mean that the highest categories must be contained in the lowest forms— which runs counter to the irreversibility of dependence and leads to an interpretation of the world "from above."

Ontology must not work with such patterns of thought. It must under all conditions cling to its own basic laws. Nor does it need such patterns. For its categorial laws render possible a very different and plausible explanation of genesis.

It is natural to assume, for instance, that at every level the particular ontological forms are susceptible to certain variations. Actually we know phenomena of this sort in all the strata. That, however, indicates the thread of instability woven into the fabric of ontological forms. If a structural type approaches the upper limit of the stratum, variants of it may pass beyond the area of structures characterizing the stratum to which the type belongs. This may have a purely negative sense. The variants, unable to survive under the categories of its own stratum, must perish. But the transgression of boundaries may also have a positive meaning, if it takes place so as to be ruled by the categories of a higher stratum. In that case the variants are seized, as it were, "from above" and become integrated into a fresh ontological context. In the place of a dissolution through instability, the stability of a higher ontological order takes effect. So an actual physical structure rendered unstable by the development of a merely dynamic equilibrium may very well become stabilized under the category of the organic equilibrium. For with it spontaneous self-regeneration and self-regulation enter in play.

The categorial groups of different ontological strata would, in the case just referred to, form stable systems of heterogeneous ontological orders. Thanks to their continuity, however, variants of typical concrete structures would be permitted to pass from one order to another. With this, the recurrence of lower categories in the higher strata would be just as compatible as the emergence of novelty in the latter. Even more harmoniously would fit in here the "being supported" of the higher strata, their resting upon the lower, and likewise the fact that they depend upon the lower strata despite all their categorial autonomy. The situation suggested here could be developed best with reference to the cases of superinformation where the lower structures with all their complexity become the matter of the higher. But in a somewhat modified form the idea of genetic transgression applies also to the relations of superimposition. For the condition of "resting upon" is the same in both cases.

This conception can be further corroborated by the reflection that within the particular ontological strata the rising scale of forms is a continuous one. We know that many-graded hierarchy best in the kingdom of organic nature, but we may trace the continuation of the series some distance both above and below the limits of organic nature. As we do so we find the strata boundaries marked only by the emergence of categorial novelty. Although this is essential from an ontological point of view, this essential fact must not be isolated from the total picture. If now in regard to the ascending order of organic forms the genetic relationship is an unmistakable fact (much though the theories concerning the dynamics of this genesis are still in disagreement), there is no reason why the same relationship should not also extend beyond the boundaries of the stratum. For these form boundaries of genesis only if the attempt is made to explain the higher ontological form by means of the categories of the lower stratum. This, however, is strictly prohibited by the laws of stratification. If, on the other hand, the transgression of boundaries involves the emergence of a categorial novelty, because the actual structures themselves must from this point on fall under the laws of a higher ontological order, then the objection to the transfer of inadequate categories to the higher form becomes baseless, and the limitations under which a genetic interpretation labors are transcended.

It must not be forgotten that this whole perspective is, after all, no more than a hypothetical interpretation, and it is not feasible to make out of it a theory to be defended on ontological grounds. Categorial analysis must keep close to the given phenomena, avoiding speculative conclusions, even those that have a certain hypothetical value. The categorial laws, within the limits of our present knowledge, can be demonstrated. The suggested schema of a genetic interpretation, on the other hand, can not be demonstrated—whether merely for the time being or not at all is a question that must be left open.

Only this one thing is ontologically important in this interpretation: It proves that the categorial laws as such undoubtedly permit a genetic view of the sequence of strata rather than preclude it, as might appear at first glance. For at the present stage of the development of the problem a theory can as a matter of principle be required to keep open the road toward the better understanding of genesis in the realm of ontological forms.

Chapter XI

The Stratification
of the Human Being

THE verification of a philosophical idea is provided in part only by the vistas which it opens. In the main it consists in rendering problems soluble. Measured by this criterion how do the ideas of stratification and categorial laws stand?

The problems under consideration here are all of a metaphysical nature. They belong to that group of problems which fall by fate to human reason because reason can neither reject them nor bring them to a complete solution. Therefore high hopes of success ought not to be raised by attempts at solving them. But although actual solutions cannot be expected, progress can still be made in dealing with these problems. They can be analyzed, and, according to whether they are attacked in the right manner or not, they may either lead to insights which clarify the situation or make the riddle still more obscure and confused.

The essential point in the laws of stratification and dependence is that with their help a number of old metaphysical problems are in part disentangled and brought closer to solution. This becomes strikingly evident as we observe how a whole group of traditional errors standing in the way of all progress dissolves in the light of these laws and makes the way free for further investigation.

One of these metaphysical problems has already been under consideration throughout the preceding discussion, because its substance is inseparable from the theme of categorial laws: the question of the unity of the world. All search after the unity of a first principle, an origin, or a world ground has proved such as to lead philosophers astray. To say nothing of the one-sidedness of their construction, philosophers who are inclined in this direction have been unable to do justice to the multiplicity of being. Nor is it sufficient to understand unity as wholeness, because thereby we do not get beyond the postulate of an incomprehensible totality. Only with the conception of a stratified order do we come to that type of unity of the real world which is suggested by the phenomena. But a concrete idea thereof can only result from a closer analysis of the laws determining the sequence of strata. For all ontic unity—no matter whether large or small—is not simplification, but organization of an underlying multiplicity.

What holds true for the unity of the world also holds, *mutatis mutandis*, for the unity of all higher structures, especially that of man. This unity, too, the old metaphysics used to oversimplify. It considered either the rational being or the natural being, trying to understand the whole of the human being as determined by either the spirit or by organic life. There is no doubt that with the spirit as point of departure a more adequate comprehension of man's specific nature was obtained. But philosophers lost sight of the ontological basis supporting spiritual life. On the other hand, it is just as evident that when bodily life was used as a starting point, this ontological basis was grasped but no understanding of the life of the spirit could be attained. Even today these two points of view are in conflict with each other in anthropology, and the strife does not seem to come to an end. And even where both sides of the human being are kept in view, theories will generally place more emphasis on one side or the other. Remnants of the Cartesian duality here seem to survive, especially where the attempt is made to overcome the duality of body and soul by the elimination of one of these two factors. The mistake consists in accepting the opposition as a point of departure, as though it were certain that we are actually confronted with a relationship of two terms.

Philosophizing in contraries is a well-known type of thought, and in the old metaphysics it was once the dominant one. It is meaningful where a gradual or continuous transition from one extreme to another is under examination. Body and spirit, however, do not shade off into each other, and there is no continuum between them. They are connected with each other rather by a third, intermediate and distinct, ontological stratum, that of psychic being.

Thus the structure of man is shown to be of many strands, and the harshness of an exaggerated contrast is done away with. The mistaken idea of an unbridgeable polarity is seen to result from an unjustified isolation of single strata. In a certain sense opposition is an even more prominent feature than it was supposed to be in former metaphysics. For naturally all four ontological strata in the human being involve certain elements of contrast. But neither can their mutual relationship be conceived in terms of contrast—they are rather linked throughout by an underlying affinity—nor can the idea of contrast serve as a schema, seeing that the relation under scrutiny involves more than just two terms.

So as a result of the concept of strata, the old conceptual schema is discarded and the interrelatedness which the latter tends to conceal becomes comprehensible. Moreover, the important thing about this is that such interrelatedness does not become comprehensible merely as a schema. Thanks to the categorial laws it rather presents itself concretely as an interplay of unrestricted dependence and autonomy taking on a special form at every one of the three strata boundaries. So it becomes possible to define more closely the type of unity peculiar to the human being. And this is achieved not by means of another schema but by an analysis of the special sort of functional relationships which interconnect the strata.

How the spirit in man transforms and directs his psychic and physical life, how it purposefully develops dispositions, enhances faculties—all this is well known. It has already been shown that this transformation leaves untouched the autonomy of the organism and of psychic life, that the spirit can create only in adapting itself to this autonomy while it has a considerable margin of liberty in regard to concrete goals. But no less pressing is the reverse question, to wit, how the particular character and tendency of the spirit, as dependent on both race and individuality, is determined by the organism.

The center of gravity of this question is in the enigmatic phenomenon of inheritability. There is, of course, no question of ontology presuming to solve a problem for which the biology of our day is as yet in no position to offer a scientifically adequate solution. For actually science knows only certain empirically established relationships between the carriers of hereditary qualities residing in the system of dispositions on the one hand and the successive evolutionary stages of the organism on the other. The underlying determining factor itself, though it is undoubtedly present, science cannot make comprehensible. And this situation coincides with the unrecognizability of the *nexus organicus* of which mention has been made in connection with the category of determination.

So far the whole problem, concerned as it is with the in-

heritance of somatic qualities alone, is an internal one of biology. It becomes an ontological problem in so far as heredity
has bearing also upon psychic and spiritual traits. Thereby the
limits of the organic are transcended, and the relationship of
the strata comes into play. If traits of character can be inherited, or if tendencies and specific talents recur in the genea-
logical sequence, explanation through reference to a purely
organic nexus of transfer will no longer do. For only the dis-
positional conditions reside in the organism, while their effect
belongs to the higher ontological strata. The germ cell with
its chromosomes is part and parcel of the spatial-material
world, while the psychic peculiarity reproduced along with
the cell is non-spatial and nonmaterial. Even if the reproduction of somatic qualities were fully explained, that of psychic
qualities would still be far from comprehensible.

Since for the time being somatic heredity is as yet unex-
plained, psychic heredity, of course, is all the more inexplica-
ble. There is, however, a question of principle concerning the
mutual relationship of the two, and this question is subject to
a categorial disquisition. For psychic qualities are not inherited
in isolation but only in conjunction with the somatic qualities
and, as it were, attached to them. And this is precisely what
all those theories which separate body and soul are insensitive
to. But the opposite theories, which completely erase the differences of the strata, fall into the opposite mistake of not
grasping the problem at all. This is the point at which the
concept of strata stands us in good stead.

The concept of strata, of course, brings help only on the
level of principles without solving the enigma of inheritance.
But the clarification of principles is not worthless. For as yet
it is not a question of explaining everything, but only of so
defining the relationship between physical and psychic processes that in spite of the heterogeneity that here prevails, a

codetermination of psychic processes by somatic ones will appear possible. Thus the ontological problem involved is methodologically analogous to the problem of a genetic interpretation of the sequence of strata. This is no mere coincidence. In both cases the problem of genesis is at stake. The point is at least to keep the way open toward an understanding of that mode of causal nexus which is sought, even though for the time being it proves undiscoverable.

The opportunity for this is afforded by the categorial laws. For these teach the dependence of the higher ontological strata on the lower strata, the former being supported and partly determined by the latter. For some of the lower categories always penetrate into the higher stratum, and this is especially true of the superimposition which takes place at the psychophysical border line. Above all it becomes clear that the modes of determination of the lower stratum are in no way limited by its upper border line. Accordingly, causal connections between physical and psychic processes can be pointed out throughout the whole gamut of relevant biological phenomena. And what holds for the causal nexus must hold as well for the organic nexus.

But should a concern for the uniqueness and autonomy of psychic life lead someone to object to the foregoing conclusion, we need only counter the objection with the reminder that this kind of dependence does not impair autonomy. There is still a sufficient number of newly emerging categories of psychic, and especially spiritual, life to ensure autonomy. Dependence is here only a partial phenomenon. The center of gravity of the higher stratum is in the laws of novelty and freedom.

On this basis it is possible to pave the way for a solution to the problem of psychic and spiritual heredity. In every individual, human nature starts its career with purely organic life, and only in this stratum is it directly connected with its ancestral line. Consciousness is not taken over from the consciousness of the parents, but is formed anew. But it is formed in a very definite dependence upon the particular growing organism. And this dependence is sufficient to serve as a basis for the heredity of faculties and dispositions of character.

Formerly in the days of the idealistic theories of neo-Kantianism, the problem of the origin of consciousness was considered an illegitimate question. But there is no use in trying to silence the philosophical desire for asking questions. The problems of philosophy spring neither from idle curiosity nor from invented difficulties. They are rather backed up by phenomena incontestable to anyone who has ever become aware of them. And behind the phenomena there is the world such as it actually is, including man such as he is. To transform the world is beyond man's power. Transform himself he may, though only in a peripheral way, not in regard to his fundamentals. Hence the substance of his problems, also the insoluble ones, is not his work but his fate. He may pass them by, but he cannot obliterate them. The genesis of consciousness from unconscious life is a fact, which in the process of the growth of every individual is brought before our eyes, regardless of whether or not we understand it. What has once been accomplished by the evolution of organisms in the grand style and on a geological time scale is here recapitulated on a small scale—according to the universal biological law of ontogenesis following at an accelerated pace the path of phylogenesis.

Thus the genesis of consciousness fits without any difficulty into the processes of organic development through which every organ and every function has to pass. It can be understood from purely biological points of view, for instance, from that of adaptation or of selection. For consciousness insures the organism of a definite superiority in the struggle for survival and so is evidently of selective value. The important point is that the autonomy of the consciousness is thereby in no way prejudiced. If, in fidelity to the facts, we regard its genesis as belonging among the morphogenetic processes of the organism, this does not mean that it is exhaustively determined by the laws of organic matter. What actually takes place is the rising of the form, with every new individual, beyond the limit of the stratum in which it originates. This again involves its integration into the higher stratum so that it then belongs under different categories.

The problem of the inheritability of psychic and spiritual characteristics does not place limitations upon the laws of novelty and freedom. On the contrary, here alone does the categorial dependence of the strata become so transparent that we can form an approximate conception of it. For here we can see what it means for the ontological form of the lower stratum to become the support of the higher form. It takes the higher form into its own process of growth without forcing upon it its particular mode of being. The organism integrates the psychic functions harmoniously into its own functions without erecting a barrier against them but also without absorbing them into its own substance. Rather, the whole animate being with its psychic life submits to an ontological law of a higher order, and the latter is sufficiently different from organic life to be able to exist together with it without friction. The result is the dovetailing, mysterious and yet so natural, of organic and psychic processes in human life. This we come to know through an immediate awareness within ourselves of the indivisible unity of the two given spheres, the inner and the outer aspects.

The nature of man can be adequately understood only as the integrated whole of combining strata and, furthermore, as placed within the totality of the same order of strata which, outside of man, determines the structure of the real world. Man cannot be understood unless the world in which he lives and of which he is a part is understood, just as the world cannot be understood without an understanding of man— that one member of the world to which alone its structure is exhibited. This exhibition is the picture of the world which philosophy sketches.

Chapter XII

Determination and Freedom

ONCE, in the metaphysics of German idealism, the problem of freedom was the driving force of philosophic research. In the first place moral freedom was meant, then freedom of the spirit as such, and, finally, the spirit was almost identified with freedom. In any case the tendency was against the universal determinism dominant in the systems of the seventeenth and eighteenth centuries. Fichte considered this determinism as a sort of serfdom of man and hailed Kant's solution of the causal antinomy as a liberation. But Kant had first revealed the whole gravity of the situation: Only a free will can be morally good and bad, and only to such a will can a moral law address itself.

But what was actually done at that time toward solving the problem of freedom? Fichte believed he could best guarantee man's freedom by negating the independence of the whole outer world with its spatiality and materiality, by letting nature, as non-Ego, be dependent on the Ego, and by pronouncing pure activity the foundation of everything. Hegel reduced nature to the spirit, considering freedom a quality attributable to spirit alone and holding that to freedom there may be added only the growing consciousness of freedom as a final achievement.

In such a conception the problem of freedom is settled in advance, without an understanding of its real difficulties. A problem of freedom exists only where a world, determined from the outset, encompasses and supports man. And this is the relationship revealed to us by the phenomena of moral life. But of all the masters of idealism, only Kant saw this relationship clearly and made it an object of inquiry. Thus he gave the problem the form of an antinomy and treated it within the context of theoretical philosophy, although the actual interest in the problem is a "practical" one.

The Kantian view of the problem has remained the standard concept, although his attempt at solving the problem was only a beginning. The problem can be finally dealt with only on the basis of ontology. For the question at issue concerns the relationship of the will to the determining powers which dominate the world from the bottom up. So what is needed here above everything else is a comprehensive view of the determining factors at the different ontological levels and, in addition, an analysis of dependence and independence characterizing their mutual relationship. For this reason the problem with its whole metaphysical weight belongs in the wider context of the laws of categorial dependence.

The shortcoming of the old theories was that they did not attack the problem of the freedom of the will within this total context, but in isolation. They did not suspect that freedom in the stratified structure of the world was a relationship recurring from rung to rung, entering into the picture wherever a group of higher determinants emerge. Nor could they see that freedom of the will, ontologically considered, is only a special case of the general autonomy of higher forms in relation to the lower ones. So they were led from the very start to a one-sided concept of the problem. Moral freedom was confronted immediately with, and understood in opposition to, causality while the intermediate determining forms, organic and psychic being, were not considered at all.

The autonomy of the organism in regard to the laws of inanimate nature is in itself no less worthy of notice than that of will in regard to the tissue of psychic motives. In both cases autonomy asserts itself as over against dependence on what is below, although of course such dependence is not to be denied either. It is no different with the autonomy of consciousness in so far as it is maintained against the determination by the supporting organism. So we have to deal with an ascending series of autonomies, and in regard to them it is clear that freedom of the will is possible only if in general there is freedom in the very dependence of the higher ontological strata on the lower.

Categorial freedom is a prerequisite of moral freedom. This, of course, does not mean that by means of the laws of dependence all pertinent special problems can be solved but, rather, that without these laws neither can a solution be achieved nor even the basic problem understood adequately. Hence the older theories, practically without exception, have resorted to metaphysical constructions with which they did not further the problem and even put themselves in the wrong.

Against every serious attempt to justify freedom of the will determinism stood like a wall. It was associated with the picture of a world in which one single chain of equal dependence ran through all the rungs of being, leaving not a single gap in which the initiative of man's spirit might have free play. Usually this chain was thought of teleologically as determined by final causes, and it was then conveniently linked with belief in predestination. For this view the whole future is predetermined with no regard to man and cannot happen otherwise, however much man is convinced that it is he who, in his little way, sets and pursues his purposes. Rarer, but less presumptuous than teleological determinism, is the causal determinism based on a scientific point of view assuming a blind historical process, indifferent to its own results. Yet here, too, the pervasive determination admits of no gap. In this view the decisions of man are effects of a causal chain of which he knows nothing, and this his ignorance is sufficient to beguile him with the mirage of freedom.

Against such varieties of determinism metaphysics was helpless. For it lies in the very nature of all serial dependence that, wherever it exists, it continues irresistibly and cannot be suspended subsequently by opposing forces. Thus the device of denying altogether the determinative nexus of the world was resorted to. Naturally this thesis, gainsaid as it was by too many well-known phenomena, could not be carried through completely. One had to be satisfied with the truncated thesis of a partial indeterminism.

In this manner room was gained for a free will. But the knot had thereby been cut rather than unraveled. Neither could the theory of gaps in the chain of dependence be reconciled with the general nature of the determinative relationships, nor was the free play that was gained sufficient for the meaning of ethical freedom. For obviously free will is by no means indeterminate will but, rather, a very determined one, although determined by itself. Self-determination, however, could not be ensured through a mere negation such as a partially suspended determination.

Thus three metaphysical theories stand opposed to each other: two types of determinism and, as a third, indeterminism opposing both the others. And right down to our own time all opinions on the question of freedom can be grouped accordingly. But from an ontological point of view it is easy to see through the errors on all three sides. Causal determinism runs counter to the law of novelty in not allowing to the higher strata their own forms of determination. Teleological determinism runs counter to the law of recurrence in transferring to the lower strata a category of the highest ontic stratum (that of purposiveness). Indeterminism finally runs counter to the basic categorial law in denying the superior strength of the lower categories. For this is precisely what is involved in the idea of interrupting the continuity of the chain of dependence in the lower strata in order to save the freedom of will.

It was Kant who first advanced on a new road in trying to understand freedom without indeterminism. With a view to this he introduced a new concept of freedom defined by him as the emergence of a positive determination of a higher order ("first inception of a causal sequence," "causality by freedom"). This freedom differs from indetermination. It is not "freedom in the negative sense" but "freedom in the positive sense." Its possibility within a causally determined world is safeguarded for Kant by the opening up, behind this world, of another world—an "intelligible" world, the world of things-in-themselves. As over against it the "empirical reality" of the given and knowable world is degraded to "appearance." Only of the latter can a pervasive causal connection be maintained. Hence room is left for the positive freedom of will without an interruption of causal chains, provided man as a moral being has an intellectual nucleus which co-operates in the decisions of the will.

The magnificence of this attempted solution has been fully appreciated by posterity. Yet posterity has not succeeded in exploiting it because the attempts to do so were too dependent on the thought patterns of transcendental idealism in which

Kant clothed his idea. This pattern, however, is the historically dated and ephemeral part of Kant's life work. Evidence
for this is the quarrel about the thing-in-itself which arose
even in the lifetime of Kant and continued down to neo-
Kantianism.

But what is permanent in Kant's treatment of the antinomy
of freedom? An answer is readily found once the principle
of the categorial laws is grasped. Freedom enters wherever a
categorial novelty enters. Free is every higher determination
which raises itself above a lower one. In a world of only one
stratum, freedom is an impossibility. In it one single type of
determination would have to rule all as a permeating nexus.
But where a higher stratum rears itself above a thoroughly
determined lower one, it brings its own determination with it
without suspending that of the lower stratum. In Kant an
intelligible world rises above the sensory one, bringing with
it its own determination (which can be grasped in the moral
law). So the effects of that higher determination in the sensory
world, instead of deriving from the latter's causal nexus, are
free from its sway.

The two strata just referred to are, it is true, not yet strata
in the sense of the new ontology. But for the problem of freedom it is sufficient that there be two strata. Thereby autonomy
becomes reconcilable with permeating causal enchainment.
For this causality does not interfere with the self-determination of the higher stratum. In this manner Kant succeeded in
justifying the freedom of the will without assuming indeterminism.

What here was gained by a stroke of genius without an
actual uncovering of the principle can now, thanks to the
idea of strata, be expressed in the form of a strict law. The
decisive point is the insight that being determined differs according to the strata and is subjected to the categorial laws of

dependence. It follows that there must also be a stratification of the forms of determination. In this stratified order, according to the law of novelty, the higher form can never be pre-determined by the lower, even where the lower recurs in the higher stratum. For (according to the laws of dependence) the lower form of determination is "indifferent" toward the higher one. At every level there is a fresh "autonomy in dependence." Looked at in this way, freedom of the will is only a special case of categorial freedom.

The mistake of the old theories consisted in a wrong alternative. It was thought that there were only two possibilities: determinism and indeterminism. The one was incompatible with freedom; the other, with the autonomy of nature. The third possibility, the stratification of determinations, was overlooked. Here, as so often in speculative theories, an incomplete disjunction was used. Hence the problem appeared hopeless. Following Kant, ontology removes the alternative. It is perfectly possible that every stratum is in its way completely determined and yet autonomous in regard to all lower determinations.

Still another error of the old theories comes to light here. It was precisely causal determinism which was generally considered especially dangerous because it was foreign to, and apparently opposed to, the purposive mode of action characteristic of the will. It was believed that it would be easier to come to terms with teleological determinism because it is akin to the will and, as it were, of its very flesh and blood. That is a disastrous illusion. If the world, from the bottom to the top, were determined teleologically, the highest form of determination would be common to all being. No higher form could rise above it, and the human will would have no determinative superiority over subhuman processes. That is to say, it would exhibit no element of superadded autonomy as over against the processes of nature; instead it would be on the same footing with these natural processes. Consequently the autonomy of a higher mode of determination would be impossible for him. The accuracy of this reasoning is further confirmed by the reflection that purposes of the more inclusive teleological processes of the world would, as superior powers, oppose all purposes of man, leaving the latter no scope at all.

In comparison, causal determinism is relatively harmless. For it allows the will its determinative superiority. The only thing incomprehensible from its point of view is how volition can assert itself amidst the seamless tissue of causal threads. As we limit the penetration of these threads to one stratum—as Kant did—room for the autonomous determination of the will is at once available. If but two things are clearly seen, first, that it is only the lower type of determination which opposes freedom and, second, that as a matter of principle the lower form can be superinformed by the higher, the ancient riddle of the reconciliation of necessity and freedom is solved.

Herewith the whole problem of freedom is, of course, not yet solved. It is tied up with still other perplexities. But the dispute about determinism is indeed settled. And this alone is a great gain.

Moreover, there is still a further partial problem which can be solved on the basis of the idea of stratification. It can be shown that the causal nexus is actually superinformable, and we can even demonstrate why it is. That is important not only for the problem of freedom but also for the determinative structure of organic processes. For even here the causal nexus is superinformed.

At every stage of the causal series there is a multiplicity of determining factors which together constitute the components of a general resultant. None of them can be omitted, for each one depends on a whole chain of causes. But new components can be added. The group of components is no closed system. Rather it is receptive to every insertion by which a codetermining element is added to the determinative whole. This is clearly reflected in the indifference of the causal nexus toward the result. For every new component must, of course, deflect the general direction.

This is why the causal nexus is superinformable whereas the teleological nexus is not. The latter's direction is fixed by the end, and every inclusion of foreign components would destroy it. Its groups of components are strictly closed. And if it were strong enough to assert itself—as it is maintained by the teleological world view in regard to the total world process —no determining factor of a different kind besides or above it could possibly develop.

Were the world ordered teleologically from below upwards, man would be unable to develop any kind of activity. His purposes would be in no position to insert themselves into the course of events. But if the world is determined causally only, and if teleological determination is the prerogative of man, he is free to deflect processes within the limits of his understanding of causality. For the causal chains admit as new components the purposes set by him, and they are given a sequence of causal effects in the same way as the indigenous components.

The three phases through which the teleological nexus develops must here be remembered. Phases one and two, the setting of purposes and the retroactive selection of means, take place in the consciousness, because only consciousness can mentally anticipate the course of time and then move backwards in the opposite direction. The third phase, however, is a real process running parallel to time: the realization of the end by the same series of means that has been traversed in the second phase, only in reversed order. Moreover this process of reality is a simple causal process. For in it the means "effect" the end. They now form a chain of causes, and they are selected with a view to just this their causal operation. Thus the causal nexus is not only a condition of the teleological process but is also included in its third phase. The fact that the first two phases precede the causal nexus is the basis of the superinformation to which the causal process is subjected by the teleological process.

This example makes very clear what is actually meant by a superinformation of lower categories by higher ones. The causal sequence recurs as a subordinate relationship, integrated into a far more complex determinative context. It is so hidden by the novelty of the latter that as a rule metaphysics has been unable to detect it, regarding teleology simply as its reversal. Categorial analysis alone can uncover the real situation: the recurrence of the causal relationship in the teleological relationship itself and its superinformability by the higher mode of determination.

It has often been affirmed that in a world of things determined causally throughout, man could not realize any ends. But just the opposite has been shown. Causal processes can be directed, because they are not committed to final purposes but proceed indifferently. It is true that they are dirigible only if man recognizes their laws and adapts himself to them. Once this condition is fulfilled they offer no active resistance to his guidance. On the other hand, if the world of things were not causally determined, man could neither direct events nor realize goals. He would be unable to select means toward his ends. For the selection is made with a view to the causal effect of the means.

The relationship of the hierarchically ordered forms of determination which has been briefly sketched here affords the basis on which depends the characteristic superiority of the spirit, its power in the world and its dominion over nature. Even though all this is not yet freedom of the will, it supplies an ontological basis on which free will depends. For will is activity, and what it intends is invariably the realization of ends. If man were denied this, his will could not make decisions in earnest. It would be condemned to ineffectual desires. Actual responsibility would not be vouchsafed it because it would lack the strength for the deed.

Thus freedom of the will and morality quite clearly depend on the categorial stratification of forms of determination and are impossible without it.

Chapter XIII

A New Approach
to the Problem of Knowledge

THERE are many metaphysical problems which can be treated in a similar way on the basis of laws of stratification and dependence. Some of them will then take on a completely fresh aspect permitting a correspondingly fresh approach.

The most important of these problems are, like the problem of freedom, on the plane of spiritual being. So the problem of historicity, for example, and together with it the problem of so-called relativism can from here be reopened and dealt with anew. For the process of history and its carrier, the human racial community, are many-stranded wholes. Hence, the phenomena revealed by history testify to an internal stratification. They form, as it were, its surface and consequently can be judged only with reference to it. But in all "relativity" the decisive question is "to what" something is supposed to be relative. If perchance truth and value are to be relative to historical periods and peoples, the real process of history will be the basis of all relatedness. It would follow that, in spite of all determination "from below," at least this process would be exempt from the relativity in question.

Instead of these mere intimations of fresh light to be thrown on this and many other problems, one single basic problem shall finally be adduced in confirmation of the main thesis— a problem in regard to which an ontologist might least be expected to bring about a change: the problem of knowledge.

The problem of knowledge has long been regarded as the basic problem of philosophy, and the theory of knowledge, its basic discipline. For philosophy itself is knowledge, its data are data of knowledge, and what it undertakes is an undertaking of knowledge. Therefore critical philosophy since Kant has considered it its main duty to explore, in preference to all other objects, the essence of knowledge. This exploration, which manifested itself already in Kant, presupposed knowledge in the other fields of research. The direction toward the object, natural to knowledge, must be reversed and turned back toward knowledge itself. That is the work of a secondary reflection which itself is subject to various errors. In any case, it presupposes the original and natural type of knowledge both as its object and the basis for reflection. In other words, it presupposes the ontological point of view. For this point of view is unreflective like that of natural knowledge whose direct continuation it is.

Another consideration must be added. Knowledge is not a mere phenomenon of consciousness, such as representation, thought, imagination. Knowledge is a relation between consciousness and its object. Thus it transcends consciousness. In that sense it is, looked upon as an act that is brought to completion, a transcendental act. Evidence of this is the fact that knowledge regards its object as "existing in itself," and this means as existing independently of its being known or of the degree to which it is known. This holds true no matter whether the object is an external or an internal one. For even a person's own conscious life proceeds independently of its being known. This transcendence extends also to the reflection of knowledge on itself. For this reflection—and in it consists epistemology—does not reflect upon itself but on the natural cognition of objects.

A third point is of decisive importance. The cognitive relationship, involving as it does the transcendent character of the relevant acts, is fundamentally an ontological relationship and, moreover, a real one. In fact it is only one among many real relationships connecting consciousness with surrounding reality. And it is by no means the first or basic one among these. Together with willing and acting, encountering and experiencing, hoping, fearing and caring, it belongs in a circle of transcendent acts with which it interlocks in life, and only at the stage of science is it raised to a position of independence. It is in these acts that the real life of man unfolds, inasmuch as it is a life in the world and bound up with the world by infinitely varied reciprocal relationships.

Nonetheless, according to its inner aspect, knowledge is a sphere of unique content, a world of perceptions, ideas, and concepts—a world forming a unified whole, set off against the outer world and admitting of no transition to it. The idea only "represents" things in the medium of consciousness, but cannot do away with them as objects—with their "objectedness." And here the ontological moment in the problem of knowledge comes into play. For the question is precisely how ideas and concepts can represent the irremovably transcendent in the medium of consciousness.

Taking as a point of departure the difference of spheres—"cognitive structures" in the consciousness (idea, concept, and the like) on the one hand and objects of knowledge on the other—the gulf between the two will seem unbridgeable.

The consequence will be either a skeptical renunciation of a solution to the question or the idealistic solution which discards the independent existence of the objects of knowledge. Both views have been advanced in a number of different versions. But even the most critical idealism runs into a difficulty. It must denounce as an illusion one of the basic phenomena of knowledge, that of natural realism which, in spite of all theories, holds us in lifelong captivity. For all knowledge "intends" its objects as existing independent of their being known.

Therefore it is imperative to choose, in the place of the difference of spheres, another starting point—one which is neutral toward all such prejudgments of a metaphysical nature. Ontology can offer an aid if we reflect that in the last analysis the cognitive relationship is itself an ontological relationship. The subject as well as the object of knowledge are ontic structures, though usually of widely different levels, and this is why in the simple knowledge of things their heterogeneity appears an unbridgeable gulf.

Thus, for the opposition of spheres, taken absolutely, the gradual difference of strata of being is substituted. While knowledge belongs to spiritual being, its objects are portioned out among all strata of being. For it is in the nature of all being that it can become an object for a knowing subject. Whether or not it does become an object depends not on itself but upon the ability of the subject to make that being its object or, to use the technical expression, to "objectify" it.

According to its mode of being, knowledge belongs to the highest stratum of the real. The character of its reality is suggested by the fact that it is something real and eminently effective in human life, that it enters decisively into all human relationships but, at the same time, that, like everything real, it has both its origin and its progression in time, existing in the individual as well as in the historical spiritual life under the form of a process. But in addition to its thus "belonging to" the level of the spirit, there is another relationship which pertains to knowledge and which concerns not its mode of being but rather its peculiar function. This function is that of "grasping" (comprehension). Moreover, in contrast to the relationship of "belonging to," this second relationship may be designated as one of "being ordered to."

Knowledge, then, is such as to be ordered not just to the highest stratum of being but to all strata, and even primarily to the lower strata. For naïve knowledge aims first at the spatial and corporeal, at visible things and living beings. This being ordered to something is nothing but the function of representation, couched in ontologically neutral terms. Thus while thought is heterogeneous in relation to things, since it belongs to spiritual consciousness, still it is ordered to things and their relationships. Idea, concept, and judgment are not ordered to each other but to something else, no matter what the position of this other factor in the hierarchy of the world might be. It is very possible that in all knowledge there might be involved a concomitant grasping of one's own spiritual self. But the knowledge of things does not consist in this concomitant apprehension nor is it dependent upon this accompaniment, and that it is so accompanied is due not to itself but to the context of existing realities through which the self is ontically bound up with things.

So the transcendence of the cognitive relationships on the one hand and the co-ordination of cognitive structures to certain objects on the other belong intimately together. Only by its being ordered to an existent does an idea become a content of knowledge and the existent, an object. This is true in its tendency at least, even where the idea either misses, or hits in part only, the real nature of the existent. For looking at the content of an idea we cannot tell whether or not it is adequate. A direct criterion of truth or error is not to be had in the realm of human knowledge.

Although the law of co-ordination is true of all knowledge, the kind of co-ordination is not the same everywhere. There is rather a wide scale of variation, beginning with simple perception and rising to intellection. The intermediate stages are varied and interlock practically everywhere. The extremes in this scale play the role of basic elements whose replicas recur throughout the totality of knowledge. So two basic types of being ordered to may be said to correspond to two types of belonging to. For within spiritual being the stages of knowledge to which these types belong are sufficiently far apart from each other to ensure them an assignment to different levels also in the stratified order. The reason is that spirit in itself is richly articulated and graduated. At its lower limit there is, still in close proximity to spiritless consciousness, perception; at its upper limit, intellection and with it the activity of research and critical self-examination.

This distinction—well known as the duality of the main kinds of knowledge—rests on a basic difference in co-ordination. In the realm of perception particular sensory qualities are ordered to certain physical events (light waves, sound waves of a certain frequency). The extreme dissimilarity between the scales of sensation on the one hand and the scales of stimuli on the other does not hinder co-ordination. For co-ordination has nothing to do with similarity. Just here the co-ordination is almost a perfect and fixed one so that the same stimuli under the same conditions are answered invariably by the same perceptions. In support of this, the sections from out of the manifold of determinate kinds of being, which are covered by perception, are enclosed in very narrow limits and cannot be arbitrarily extended.

Of a completely different type is the co-ordination regnant in intellection. It adheres to the universal in being, to its uniformity and its conformity to laws. So, in the final analysis, it depends on the categories. Its function is known under the name of the a priori in knowledge. In the knowledge of the real it never exists separately but keeps within the frame of experience throughout. But the insight which it affords surpasses experience because the universal as such cannot be experienced. The crucial point for this kind of co-ordination is whether the categories of knowledge correspond to the categories of being. Only if these two coincide can thought hit off being.

That such a coincidence, even though not a total one, exists is suggested by a series of important and well-known facts. The best known of these is the fact that what has come to be known in principle and universally is then progressively confirmed in experience and in the practice of life. Ontologically, this involves the recurrence of ontic categories of lower strata in the structure of the intelligent spirit. Thus in the understanding, in so far as it is concerned with calculation, the categories of quantity recur; in the knowledge of nature, spatiality, temporality, substantiality, causality, reciprocity, and many others recur. Indeed, the situation is such that the whole co-ordination of the higher level, involving a priori cognition and comprehension, is rendered possible by the recurrence of the categories of the spirit.

Looked at from the point of view of the laws of stratification in the area of thought, this recurrence is readily understood. It is no more than a special case of the penetration of lower categories into the higher strata. But the penetration itself is here of a very special sort. For those categories of nature reappear in the spirit not as categories of its own reality but only as categories of its own content. Knowledge itself as a spiritual function and a transcendent act is far from being something spatial, substantial, or even quantitative. Rather it has its own categories which are totally foreign to the lower ontic strata. Among these are the separability of the content from the act, its indifference in regard to the individual subject, its "intentionality" and objectivity, and, last but not least, the category of co-ordination itself, inextricably bound up as it is with transcendence as an element of the act.

But the assertion that the lower categories recur in the content of knowledge means something completely different. There they form the structural moments of the cognitive structure (of idea, concept, and so forth), and within this structure they must necessarily recur if knowledge is to be authentic, that is "true," knowledge. For the cognitive structure is co-ordinated to the cognitive object, its purpose being to represent the latter. It has cognitive value only in so far as it "makes present" (represents) the ontic structure of the object in the consciousness, and it can do so only if it bases itself on the same categories as the object.

What takes place here is a sort of reduplication of the categories in the cognitive relationship. The same categories confront each other in the object and the subject: in the object as categories of the real, in the subject as categories of content only. And this relationship obviously belongs to the essence of the cognitive spirit in the same way as act, transcendence, and being ordered to.

So far the situation seems quite simple. But the mere duplication will not do. And this critique must attempt to discover the limits of identity between ontological and epistemological categories by means of a differential analysis for each single category. The space and time of our experience, in which we become aware of material objects, are not identical with the real space or real time in which these things move. They are neither infinite nor strictly continuous nor uniform, but deformed in accordance with the human perspective and circumscribed by very vague outlines. The modification is not equally apparent in all categories. But in most of those which we can grasp at all at least vestiges of such modification are noticeable.

If we now remember that the a priori element of knowledge depends on the identity of cognitive and ontic categories and that the limits of this identity are also the limits of apriorism, the modification of this recurrence becomes a matter of considerable importance. For epistemologically it becomes a real task to define with precision for every particular case the deviation from the ontic category. Obviously this cannot be done summarily for all categories but only by detailed analysis, the factor of deviation from the corresponding category of the real being a different one in every cognitive category. Categorial identity seems most complete in the realm of quantitative categories. Hence it is natural to conclude that this accounts for the exactness of mathematical knowledge. But as this concerns one aspect of reality only and plays a leading role in the sciences of inanimate nature alone, no further consequences of more general scope follow. In the other fields of knowledge the ontic and the cognitive categories are clearly far apart from each other, and the farther apart they are, the higher the objects of knowledge would seem to be within the hierarchical stratification of the real.

In the way of a neat ontological analysis of this type—that is, of an epistemologically differentiated investigation of the categorial situation—almost nothing has been done so far. The problem, however, has become urgent as a result of the emphasis placed on the ontological aspect of epistemology. It is to be expected that its treatment, once philosophy attacks it seriously, will develop into a whole science with its own methods and its own division of labor.

What can be accomplished by means of such an investigation is of extreme importance for all scientific knowledge, but especially for philosophical knowledge. It consists in nothing less than progressing along the road opened up by Kant's *Critique of Pure Reason*. At any rate this is so if we strictly interpret the *Critique* as what it was originally intended to be: a critique of a priori knowledge.

It has been shown above how in still another respect the new ontology points in this direction. Formerly, the problem was that of the right limitation to be placed upon the use of categories in their application to objects of experience. Kant had defined this limitation only in a general way for all categories. But it has now become clear that for every single category there is needed a particular limitation to certain fields of objects, that this limitation is not simply defined by the limits of an ontic stratum (for there is the recurrence of lower categories in higher strata), and that, consequently, there is required, for the definition of the limits of legitimate application of every particular cognitive category, an ontological inquiry which finds out just how far and with what modifications the corresponding ontic category reaches into the higher strata.

But now, in addition, a second requirement in the way of a differential categorial analysis is to be added. Even within the legitimate sphere of application of a cognitive category there are certain limits to its competence, because of the fact that in content it is only partly congruent with the corresponding ontic category. Both in life and in the majority of sciences this limitation of congruence—the "categorial difference"—plays no significant role. However, in regard to the ultimate problems of the limits and foundations of sciences in general, and in philosophy in particular, it does play a very decisive role. For here the sphere of problems extends beyond the limits of the sphere of experience to which the categorial apparatus of human knowledge is adjusted. This adjustment consists in categorial identity; it is, however, but a limited one. Hence philosophical knowledge must have recourse to a critique of the a priori elements in it, and this critique must attempt to discover for the single categories the limits of the identity of ontological and epistemological categories by means of a differential analysis.

How far we may progress along this road cannot, of course, be predicted. But it is not impossible that speculative questions about the limits of different fields of knowledge, as well as questions of a sort that lead to antinomies, may well be unraveled. To the first type belong those philosophic categorial problems to which theoretical physics has led; to the second type belongs the much-debated problem of truth in the context of philosophical relativism. In both cases the presuppositions concerned are so fundamental that they are involved even in the propositions designed to eliminate them. This absurdity might perhaps be removed by recognition of the fact that an elimination in terms of epistemological categories need not involve an elimination in terms of ontological ones.

Of a more general significance than all problems of limits is the problem of the dual co-ordination involved in all knowledge of the real. It is concerned with the knowledge about "true" and "untrue" and, consequently, with the ancient problem of a criterion of truth. If only one form of co-ordination existed in human knowledge, then, on account of the transcendence in the cognitive relation, an awareness of the adequacy or inadequacy of an idea in relation to an existent could either not develop at all or would have to be a deceptive one. But since there are two forms of co-ordination sufficiently heterogeneous and independent of one another, the fact that they agree in what they yield is a valid testimony of adequacy. And this testimony can gain in value by the growth of the content of knowledge.

This idea is an old one. It lies at the basis of all tendency toward the confirmation of a priori insights through experience. But it first comes into its own if the phenomenon of transcendence in the epistemological relationship is understood as an ontological relationship and if behind the opposition of subject and object the superimposition of ontological strata is recognized. On the basis of transcendental philosophy this was impossible. The reflective character of the purely epistemological approach here defeats its own purpose. Only by virtue of the ontological approach, for which the subject is an existent among existents, can the duality of the branches of knowledge be understood as a fundamental difference in co-ordination. Only thereby does the co-operation of the two achieve the power to justify in principle the claim to transcendent truth.